I0438279

If Only . . . Is Just If Only

If Only . . . Is Just If Only

Dorothy Rudzi C. Wright

Copyright © 2009 by Dorothy Rudzi C. Wright.

ISBN: Softcover   978-1-4415-6671-3

All rights reserved. No part of this book may be reproduced or transmitted in
any form or by any means, electronic or mechanical, including photocopying,
recording, or by any information storage and retrieval system, without permission
in writing from the copyright owner.

This book was printed in the United States of America.

To order additional copies of this book, contact:
Xlibris Corporation
1-888-795-4274
www.Xlibris.com
Orders@Xlibris.com
66442

DEDICATION

I would like to dedicate my book to my grandfather (Nhamo),
my grandmother (Matema), my brother Emmanuel
and my kid sister Jane – LOVE YOU AND MISS YOU – REST IN PEACE...

ACKNOWLEDGEMENT

I WOULD LIKE TO acknowledge and give special thanks to my parents who molded me into who I am today – the wisdom to distinguish between right and wrong – know and love God and to remember that a good name is better than riches – last but not least for this untold story.

I would like to thank my brother Andrew for his support and help in completing the book and my sister Gladys for being there when I needed her sisterly-elderly advice.

Special thanks to friends that supported me financially, mentally and physically – namely, Lora Allred, Laurie Masenhimer, Marcie McReynolds, Debbie Nelson, First United Methodist Church and not forgetting my Nephew Tapiwa.

I would also like to acknowledge University of Phoenix for making me believe that it is never too late to learn by nudging me forward with their excellent teachers.

Last but not least; Thank you XLIBRIS CORPORATION for making my seven years dream come true by publishing this book. Your team is very professional and easy to work with – again, thank you.

CHAPTER ONE

THE FIRST THING that caught your eyes when you arrived at the Buffalo Horn Farm was the sore sight of the worker's compound, it was a neglected, impoverished and mosquito infested place comprising of over hundred poorly erected mud huts housing approximately 200 families that slaved and toiled on the massive unknown hectares of land for a bag of Corn-meal, a pack of beans and a jug of milk per week, not forgetting the free accommodation if one can call them that. The farm foreman who was forty two at the time had a most peculiar name; Spinach. Spinach was a stout, 5.7 foot tall balding black man with puffy cheeks and a forehead that at a quick glance one would think he had a golf ball stuck to his face. His nose was as wide as his mouth with big brown eyes that were not charming to look at. The description says it all but to put it in a simple way – he was ugly. He considered himself the chosen child of Israel because as a foreman Spinach was living in a three roomed, brick walled, and asbestos roofed structure, erected in the middle of the Compound hovels with his wife and daughter.

The house and Spinach himself stood out like sore thumbs amongst the peasants. The owner of the farm had deliberately erected the house in the middle of the compound to make it easy for his watch dog Spinach to sniff out any gossiping or complaints in and around the compound. Spinach was worse than a double-edged sword because during the night when nearly everyone was nursing wounds sustained through the rough field toil, Spinach the foreman or 'Tsvukukuviri' (two faced) as he had been dubbed, would mix with the worn out folks, ears as switched on as Antenna's, to record any traces of complaints from his fellow black workers. On occasions, some laborers would be too tired to notice his presence and begin to brand the boss with all sorts of names ranging from 'oppressor' to anything they deemed fit. That same instant, Spinach would scamper off in the dark, slithering like a boom slang to spill all the gossip to boss-man Hamilton, whose reaction would be just as equally swift. He'd pay the gossiping party a nasty visit; a visit that sometimes left funerals and burials behind. Stewart did not hesitate to use his .38 special gun or just kick the daylight out of whoever crossed his path; an act that gave him one of his many nicknames 'Shangu' (Shoes) owing to the impulsive use of his boots in kicking anyone and anything in sight for no apparent reason. This treatment to him was a way of suppressing any rebellious ideas in his workers and it paid dividends because most of his workers had been reduced to voiceless zombies – thanks to Spinach!

Stewart Hamilton was the only child born from a crossbreed of a Dutch mother and an Irish father. The parents had moved from England to Northern Rhodesia before he was born and so Stewart was an Irish by origin and a Northern Rhodesian by birth. At the age of eighteen, after completing his A-Level at St. Peters Secondary School, Stewart left Northern Rhodesia to study Law at a University in London (name unknown). Six years two months from the day of Stewart's departure, both Stewart's parents were murdered by two burglars that broke into their home at the Buffalo Horn Farm and stole goods worth more than 15 thousand pounds and hell broke loose; police and police dogs were brought to the scene and every peasant on the farm was an immediate suspect. Spinach, wanting to be on the good side with the police gave a false statement implicating some of his fellow workers whom knowing very well were innocent wanted to get them into trouble because he simply disliked them. The five men were badly beaten with police buttons and forced to confess before being loaded into the police car and taken to remand prison to await their fate.

As luck would have it or shall we say God was on the accused five men's side because within that same week, the two men who had broken into the Hamilton's home where arrested. The two men were found in possession of the stolen goods after they tried to sell one of the stolen items. During that time there were certain items that no African would posses and so if found with such expensive items the police would need an explanation or a letter from your employer to prove that you were given as a gift or other. The two men tried to explain their way out but could not come up with a convincing story and after severe beatings and torture one of them confessed and led the police where the rest of the items were hidden. Two days later and without a trial the two men were used as an example and a warning to anyone that would commit a similar crime by executing them in public after humiliation of nakedness, cutting of fingers one at a time and asking the parents of both men to eat the fingers whilst the crowd cheered, and then finally gunned down.

Stewart was devastated at the loss of his parents; he was five months short of completing his Law Degree and was looking forward to coming home with his new bride, Gail who was pregnant at the time and their son Duncan who was two years old. Stewart being the only child inherited the entire estate of his parents and after the burial decided to commit to farming instead of pursuing his career in Law. Farming was not one of Stewart's interests because even though his parents were farmers, he spent most of his time at a boarding school and overseas. The urge to punish every black person for the death of his parents was reason enough for him to decide to change course and become a full time farmer and knowing he would have Spinach to help him execute his decisions sent a surge of excitement in his veins, but hate the blacks as much as he did, Stewart knew he needed them for the purpose of cheap child and adult labor.

Everything turned for the worst at the farm from the first day Stewart took over the affairs of the farm. All workers were summoned to attend a meeting that stipulated new policies to be followed that included starting work at 4 am and ending at 6 pm (Monday to Saturday with only 30 minutes break in between instead of the old 6 am to 5 pm with three intervals in between. Sunday was the only day that they would work from 4 am to noon. Spinach, who could not speak proper English except chilapalapa (mixture of Shona the native language and English), was the interpreter and where he did not understand would put in his own words that included giving himself more power and adding fear in the already nervous peasants. At the end of the meeting there was silence as everyone tried to in visualize what was to come, for Spinach it was the beginning of better days.

Stewart was not a frightening figure to look at because he was not muscular but of medium built with a height of 5.3 feet. He had beautiful cheek bones with dimples and a line on his chin, a well maintained moustache and hair cut that was army or police style – short and well trimmed. The only feature that subtracted from his otherwise handsome face was his icy cold eyes that brought shivers to any peasant unfortunate enough to see them because that did not happen often unless there was trouble and when that happened one would expect either kicks from his steel front padded boots or a nasty tragic shot from his .38 police special gun that he wore around his waist at all times. The unfortunate part was that, to be able to avoid crossing paths with Stewart, you had to lick Spinach's feet by treating him like royalty.

Stewart capitalized on the natural farming instincts of the Mashona people who made up the bulk of his labor-force, to emerge as one of the most successful white farmer of the British colony. He acquired the best of the best studs and that added to his fortune so much that half of the vast land was now strictly for breeding cows, goats, pigs and sheep whilst the other half was for tobacco, corn, cotton, beans and sunflower. The name of the farm was changed from the Buffalo Horn to the Seven Stud farm (not sure why). His father's once struggling farm, had blossomed into a multi-million dollar agricultural establishment, known for its bumper tobacco harvests, and a variety of export produce. He also diversified into dairy farming and was raking in thousands in foreign currency through his produce. By this time at the age of 45 his two sons were in their twenties. Duncan, who was the older of the two sons, spent very little time at the farm because his interest was in hotel management and his father had bought him a hotel in Whilshire which he was running and had turned into a five star hotel where top special delegates from other countries including presidents would stay during their visit to Northern Rhodesia. The younger son Sidney was interested in farming and so lived on the farm with his parents. He was in charge of marketing and accounting.

⚜

It was a common feature to see the Compound completely deserted during the week because every family member of the peasants was expected to work except for toddlers but that was no reason not to go to the field, if you had an infant you would work with the baby on your back and those a year to five years would be assigned a girl between 8-10 years to baby sit under a fig tree that provided enough shed in the 110 degrees African heat whilst the parents slaved in the various areas of the farm. Breasts feeding outside the 30 minutes break spelt instant punishment and as such infants would wail until their wind pipes accumulated dust.

Nyasha (Mercy) a first time mother could not stand hearing her infant cry and so whenever Spinach was out of sight she would sneak to the fig tree, feed her baby and run back to the cotton field whilst others kept watch for Spinach. After a couple of weeks of the same routine Nyasha had the shock of her life when out of the blue Spinach emerged and stood before her. Spinach not able to contain his rage and not caring about the baby in her arms, grabbed Nyasha by her bony shoulder and shoved her so hard that she stumbled over the baby that had slipped from her arms and landed head first to the ground. Nyasha panicked when she fell and turned to see her baby motionless and bleeding through the mouth. She crawled towards her baby ignoring the pain she felt in both knees after the fall. When she picked the baby up she freaked out and started screaming hysterically. The scream attracted other peasant's attention and they came running to see what was going on. Spinach disappeared into the long corn afraid that they might attack him after what he had just done. Her husband was the first to arrive on the scene but it was too late – the baby had died. The young couple was in so much anguish after the loss of their only child. Unfortunately, there was nothing anyone could do but to keep the pain bolted up inside them; like all other incidences that were going on whilst the police pretended not to know and those that tried to report ended up being the victims of fate – worse of all was the fact that pain and suffering was being initiated by one of their own SPINACH. None of the workers dared breathe out anything to offend Stewart's most faithful pet Spinach. They knew better than to commit suicide that way. They hated the foreman's guts but had to force smiles on their hard beaten faces each time he wobbled past them. He was the boss's mirror, always watching Stewart's back for him. Unfortunately, on several occasions he would create stories that were untrue just to get praise from Stewart that he was doing his job well without considering the repercussion on those that he was reporting.

Stewart's name spread beyond ordinary borders to the very chambers of the Northern Rhodesian Parliament where reports were received of his disregard of human life through some white Missionaries. The countless times he had massacred families of his labor force then simply riding out on his horse to drag in another family to replace the eliminated one from the nearest Bantu-Stan. Those killed would be buried in shallow graves like dogs and quickly forgotten about. However, whatever or how much the Missionaries Human Rights Organizations, or International Bodies for Justice and Peace protested, the Government let it ride as trivial because Stewart spelt money, power and influence. It was a waste of time and money to try and prosecute Stewart because he was the law. After all, there was very little care, if any, for Africans in particular during these worst segregated times by the British Colonial rule under Cecil Rhodes, Welensky and later Ian Smith. Clear beer was strictly for whites only and if one saw a black person in any office or hotel – they were cleaners, waiters, or cooks for very little wages that barely sustained a family of three. Those that worked in hotels would scrap up leftovers to feed their families but if caught would be treated to severe beating with a sjambouk, so the government did not really care how Stewart disciplined his so-called human game as long as he was filling their coffers with wealth.

CHAPTER TWO

N HAMO WAS BORN in Hartley but at the age of six after the death of his father, his mother was taken in as a wife by her brother-in-law who worked and lived at the Buffalo Horn farm, this was customary law. Two years later his mother also died, word has it that even though she agreed to be married to the brother-in-law, she missed her husband and it is that stress and depression that killed her, others thought she committed suicide but nothing was confirmed. Nhamo continued to live with his uncle who cared for him as much as his own three children. When he turned 19 there was an arranged marriage between Nhamo and a 16 years old girl from one of the families within the compound. Since there was no money to exchange as dowry, Nhamo had to go hunting during the night and bring three beasts to give to the in-laws as dowry. One would be prepared for the guests to feast during the ceremony, the other would be shared among the girl's relatives and one would be for the girl's direct family. Meat was preserved by drying it in a form of biltong and cooked on special occasions such as birth of a child, visitors or just to appease the ancestral spirits.

Nhamo was blessed with four children, Kuda, the oldest at nine years old, followed by Rutendo, seven years old (both boys) and a set of twin girls who were four years old but at 28 he looked 40 due to the harsh weather and being in the field day in and day out from the time he was able to walk. His light complexion had been burnt down by the scorching heat and so he looked pitch black around his exposed skin such as the face arms legs and other parts of the body that his rags could not cover, but the rest of the body had his original light brown color. His left hand was deformed from birth but that did not stop him from doing his duties. He was a very soft spoken person liked by all because even though they all worked tirelessly he would volunteer to help others finish their chores to help them avoid confrontation with Spinach.

One morning as Nhamo and his family got ready to go to the tobacco field, he could not help wondering why he felt so uneasy and weak as if he was getting some kind of fever. As they sat to eat their usual breakfast of corn porridge mixed with home-made peanut butter, his wife who had noticed the worry on his face asked if something was wrong, Nhamo, looked at his family as if deep in thought then with a shrug and a grin explained the feeling which according to him was the same feeling he felt the night before his mother died and so hoped it was not a sign of bad news to come. His wife reminded him that working and living under Spinach and Stewart anything was possible but they laughed it off and Nhamo picked one of his daughter whilst the wife carried the other twin and the family headed to the their daily jobs with the boys right behind playfully.

At sundown, feeling exhausted, the family left the fields with the rest of the peasants but instead of returning to their compound, Spinach had summoned everyone to meet under the fig tree where all meeting took place because he had an announcement to make. He took his own sweet time to get there with no care that these peasants needed to get to their homes and prepare meals and rest within the few hours they had before they had to get up again for another day's work. Finally, after almost an hour, he emerged from behind an out building and came waltzing forward, a mug of clear beer in one hand. Nhamo shuddered with loathing as a young boy, barely in his teens rushed forward carrying a wooden stool for Spinach. Settling his frame down and his mug next to his feet, he asked everyone that was over seventy five to stand up. There were over twenty men and women that stood up and Nhamo's uncle and his wife were among them. Spinach told them that they were no longer needed on the farm and so had two days to pack their rags and move out because Boss Stewart was bringing in fresh blood to take their places. "Where are they going to go? This is the only place they know" the peasants shouted in disbelief. "You have two choices, to leave in two day or be on a shooting squad" Spinach retorted, with no care for the poor old folks. There was so much wailing that even those that were not impacted could not help shedding tears. One old woman in desperation threw herself on Spinach's feet begging for mercy, but he ignored her. The old woman got to her feet and looking at Spinach, said "Child, know your roots and remember that whatever you do, the spirits are watching – feast now whilst you . . ." Her sentence was cut short by Spinach's outburst and a slap across the face that sent her off balance. "I am boss-man Stewart's son and so nothing will befall me and in case I did not mention, no one that is below the age I just mentioned is to leave the farm – that is that." Spinach shouted angrily. As if what he had just said and done was not enough, a little girl that was running around playfully accidentally knocked his beer mug spilling all the contents. Those that saw what had just happened froze with eyes transfixed on Spinach with a dreadful anxiety of what was about to happen (knowing Spinach the way they did). The crowd didn't have to wonder for long because almost instantly, Spinach grabbed the little girl and slammed a clenched fist into her face knocking her unconscious. Nhamo who happened to be sitting way in the back heard his wife's scream amidst the commotion of trying to resuscitate the little girl whilst Spinach stood towering over the poor girl. Infuriated beyond control, Nhamo swung into action, he lugged at Spinach and began connecting vicious blows into the stout fellow's face, by the time he was through, and the foreman was one bloody heap with two broken ribs and a fractured arm. The peasants were happy that finally Spinach had got what he deserved but at the same time they knew Nhamo was in big trouble and he knew it too. He knew that every second he spent at the farm was a disadvantage and so he quickly packed his little belongings and left the farm compound with his wife and children, heading for the unknown. Unfortunately, the pace was not as fast as he would have wanted due to his pregnant wife and the two little girls and leaving them was not an option because even though Stewart did not know who was who in the compound, his sniff dog Spinach knew.

Stewart got wind of the incident almost two hours later and was spitting fire with rage as he mounted his horse to go in search of "the beasts" as he called them with a bright spotlight attached to the front of his helmet. The night was so dark that moving in the forest was almost impossible for the already tired and hungry family. Suddenly, they saw the flash light coming from a distance and Nhamo knowing there was no way out told his wife to take the children and hide in the bushes and let Stewart deal with him alone but the wife refused and the two girls clung to their mother. Rutenda tried to pull them away so as to save them from whatever was about to happen but the more he pulled the more they wailed. Nhamo grabbed his boys and gave them a bear hug, in a quivering voice he said "Do not worry about us we are going to be in a better place with those that went before us, we will protect you and if you feel scared remember we will be there; just promise me that you will take care of each other and that you will stop the two devils Spinach and Stewart one way or another – run along now as fast as you can." After a bit of hesitation the boys held their mother who was sniffling and all she was able to say was "Remember all that I have taught you about God." As the boys walked away also sniffling, their mother broke down uncontrollably. Barely had the boys branched off into the bush that a light flashed directly were the family stood like cornered rabbits. Kuda and Rutendo were not spared the horror of watching from their hiding place as Stewart ruthlessly gun down their family; Kuda screamed and Rutendo quickly covered his mouth asking him to hush up. Stewart heard the sound and began moving towards them but out of nowhere came an impala at full speed as if being chased by a lion and Stewart must have thought that is what he had heard because he turned his horse and rode off leaving the four corpses for the wild animals to feast; rode with pride that he had accomplished his mission – a stint he was used to in all the years of his reign.

The boys waited until the light had disappeared into the night before emerging from their hiding place and crawling over to see if by chance someone survived the massacre but there was dead silence – Stewart saw to it that none of them lived to tell the tale. The two boys gathered fresh branches from near by trees and covered the dead bodies before taking off into the bush with nothing but one bow and arrow and a spear that their father had given them. Rutendo, unlike his older brother was a brave boy despite his age; the loss of their family was painful but Rutendo knew that if they were to survive they had to flee as far away from the farm as possible. So he led his elder brother who was hysterical forward, telling him to be a man because being alone they had to be and act like men. Days to weeks they wondered the forest tirelessly, surviving on wild berries and locusts but how they evaded the man-eating beasts of the wild, no man could ever tell. They had been in the bush for over a month and unable to go on with their half naked bodies full of cuts, they sat down to rest and fell into a deep sleep.

A German couple who had set camp for Archeology Research found the shredded forms. The couple stood and watched the boys whom at first they thought were dead but then saw the exposed bellies moving up and down; a sign that they were breathing. "Where could they have come from in this thick forest far from society?" the woman wondered loudly. Rutendo heard the voice and opened his eyes and seeing the couple standing before them, he screamed with fright and the scream woke Kuda who after seeing the couple also screamed, they tried to run away but they had no strength so they sat there wide eyed and shaking like leaves. The couple assured them that it was okay but there was a language barrier and so the boys had no idea what the couple was saying. Knowing that the conversation was not going anywhere, the couple held each boy's hand and led them to their camp.

The fear and desperate need to escape was replaced by disbelief and a feeling of being dead and in paradise. Rutendo could not believe that this white couple had just given them food in the most beautiful plates they had ever seen. After feeding them, the lady took her perfumed soap, towel and a basin and gave both boys a good scrub. Their rugs were replaced by the lady's t-shirts and shorts which because of their bony frames had to be tied with a string so that they don't fall off. Sleeping arrangements were no different; they all slept in one cozy tent.

The couple made a few changes to their routine in order to accommodate the boys. The husband went on with the research whilst the wife stayed behind to try and teach the boys how to speak, read and write English, she so much wanted to know more about the boys and where they came from because she wanted to make sure they would be safe after she and her husband left for Germany which was in a couple of weeks. Rutendo and Kuda felt that if there was paradise, this was it because they did chores only when they felt like it and the best time of the day was when they had to sit with the white lady whom they had grown so fond of that it was like having their own mother once again. Rutendo who even though younger was also the brightest, he learnt much faster than Kuda. He was able to make sentences that made sense even though they were in broken English.

One evening as they were having dinner, the woman decided to tell the boys about their just ended research and that they would be returning back to Germany in two day and that they needed to know where Kuda and Rutendo's family was so as to take them there before they left. "Moder and fader kill by lion no famiry; priz we go with you to gereman" Rutendo said, almost shouting in desperation but not wanting to mention Stewart and the farm. Kuda even though did not quite understand what all this meant; he sensed that this beautiful couple was leaving soon. "Pruriz no go we . . ." he broke down and began to sob because the picture of his family came flooding back in his mind and the thought of having to lose the most precious couple that had treated them as their own and the likelihood of being returned to the farm was more than he could bear. The lady became emotional too. She pulled both boys to her and held them tightly and with tears running down her cheeks to Rutendo's back, promised to make sure they were in safe hands before leaving for Germany. The following day was very somber as they packed all the belongings into their rented 4 x 4 wheel drive truck. All the boys could do was trust that this lovely couple that had taken care of them as their own children with unconditional love would see to it that they were safe from Spinach and Stewart. During the six hours drive, the excitement of being in a truck for the first time in their entire lives brushed aside the fear and anxiety of where they were heading to and what was to become of them. True to their word, the couple drove to a suburb in Whilshire were they knew about a Catholic Orphanage manned by Father James whom they had met at one of the conferences that they attended and at which they were sending donations each year in support of the good work the orphanage was doing. On arrival, the couple discussed the welfare of the boys and promised to double their donations so that the boys would be able to attend school and asked Father James to keep them posted on the boy's progress. The two boys stood and watched the truck until they could no longer see the dust trail "God take care of them where-ever they go and I pray that you bless them with children" Rutendo whispered before following Father James who had beckoned them to follow him into the building.

The orphanage was in desperate need for donations but because of the segregation that was going on in the country, very few organizations or individuals donated toward the orphanage because it catered for minorities. Due to poor funding, it was not up to the normal or required standards but at lest it provided shelter and food for those that got the chance to walk through the doors after surviving the harsh political/apartheid arena. Father James was very pleased to have the two boys, especially with the wonderful couple promising to send more donations to help the orphans. Most of the children were from the streets, where every now and again Father James would drive around the streets and take the most desperate kids off the streets and give them a warm place to sleep and good meals. "God will provide" was his theme. Rarely, did he do anything special for himself, it was all about others. One day the volunteers at the orphanage decide to surprise him with a party on his 80th birthday. The first thing he said was that they should have used the money to buy more food for the orphanage, but the good thing is he enjoyed it and was grateful that they had honored him in such a special way. When anyone made a comment on how young he looked even though he was eighty, he would say jokingly "those that have found favor with God never get old." He had faithfully served at the orphanage for over 27 years and was a perfect person to run the orphanage because he was a very compassionate humble man. His commitment to the orphanage was from his heart because sometimes he could be seen sitting on one of the dilapidated swings with an orphan in his lap singing him or her to sleep. He was hated by those that felt that he was giving these black children too much attention so much that on one occasion, teenagers broke into the orphanage and vandalized, beat and injured eleven orphans; it's a wonder that there were no tragedies. Father James who was not fazed by the attack continued to do good with his team of volunteers who were just as caring as him.

A week had gone by and the two boys were settling in very well, the little English they had been taught by the German couple made them stand out among other orphans who could not speak a word of English. This did not go unnoticed by Father James; he saw their potential and decided he would send them to a Catholic Mission Boarding School that was affiliated to the orphanage. Each year the orphanage was granted three scholarships for any three orphans of Father James' choosing to attend school at the Mission. He had five months to get to know the boys better before the beginning of school in the following year.

One fine day, he summoned the two boys to his office. The first thing he wanted to know was about their background; where had they come from before being found by the German couple and also what their names where. He was getting tired of calling them 'Pikinini one' and 'Pikinini two' (small boy one and two). Afraid of being identified, Rutendo who was outspoken and the brighter of the two gave his name as Shungu and Kuda as Garikayi. He also explained how they became orphans even though they did not give him the full details about who had killed their parents or where they were staying at the time. Father James could see the pain in the eyes of Rutendo (now Shungu) as he told his story and even though he could tell that there were loopholes in the story, he did not push further but knew that some day he would get the real truth. Father James told them his decision to send them to school and the pain in the big brown eyes turned to sparks of excitement, Shungu unable to contend his joy jumped straight into Father James' arms then quickly backed off ashamed. Father James looked at him and without saying a word just smiled.

Father James registered both Shungu and Garikayi at the School and personally drove them there. Shungu and Garikayi were so excited and they looked very ready for school in their second-hand khaki shorts and shirts and a note book and pencil each, the only thing that was lacking were shoes but they did not care. They were not sure of what to expect on arrival but from stories that they had been told by Father James Shungu was so ready but Garikayi had his own reservations. On arrival, they saw hundreds of children ranging from maybe six to twenty years old and the joy was that except for a handful none of them had shoes and most uniforms had had their time. Garikayi even though being the oldest, was not doing too good in schoolwork such that Shungu moved a class above him. The difference between the two boys was obvious. Shungu was keen to learn as much as he could and he hoped that one day he could become a teacher. Garikayi on the other hand had no particular goals and to make matters worse he had joined a group of friends that were just as lazy and on one occasion he was nearly expelled for getting into a fight with one of the students.

The mission school had been under construction for years with no hope of completion due to lack of funds and so classrooms were not to standard. The black boards were almost falling off and sometimes the teachers ran out of chalk and would use whatever they could to write on the board. The dilapidated desks that were suppose to be for each student were shared by eight students on each with all kinds of home-made stools such as 20 litre tins, carved wood or simply sit on the dusty floor. The domes were just as bad, no beds but mats and one blanket each. To be creative and keep warm some students would sleep together so as to have one blanket for the bottom and one to cover. Twenty-five thatch structures with no roofs could be seen over one hundred yards away, they were Blair toilets (a deep hole dug and used as a toilet) with enough room for bathing as well; used by the entire school. There was no running water and so water used for cooking and bathing came from the six wells that were dug by the students as one of the projects.

Shungu and Garikayi had been in school for four years three months and during that time they spent the school holidays at the orphanage, which was the only home they had and knew. Shungu was busy studying for his first exam to enable him to get a junior certificate (grade seven) whilst Garikayi had another year to go before he could write the exams. On the day of the exams like any other day, all students assembled in the makeshift school hall for a briefing from the headmaster and being a catholic mission school would have thirty minutes of church service before being dispersed to their designated classrooms.

The headmaster was just about to wish the students luck in their exams when there was an interruption by eleven black gunmen who claimed to be freedom fighters. The entire school was held hostage by five of the nine men whilst the other two dragged the headmaster to the office where they forced him to open the little safe that had just a few dollars because banking had just been done the day before. The other two force-marched two teachers to the kitchen were they filled bags with foodstuff and anything they thought they could use. They returned back to the hall with the loot and the guns still pointing at the headmaster and the two teachers. Even though there were no benches, everyone was ordered to sit down and in a split second no one was left standing for fear of being killed. After a short tete-a-tete the gunmen began to separate the students in two groups; one group of almost 100 students was ordered out of the assembly hall whilst the rest were asked to remain in the hall. Garikayi was among the ones ordered out of the hall. The teachers were also separate. The headmaster and the two teachers who were white, were ordered to go outside and the black teachers where asked to sit down with the rest of the students. The two gunmen kept watch in the hall whilst the rest went outside.

It was nerve wrecking for everyone inside because they could not tell what was going on outside. Those outside did not know what their fate was either but they didn't have to wait much longer. The three white men were gagged and one of the men who seemed to be the leader of the gang announced that they were going to execute them as revenge on all innocent black people that had been murdered. As for the students they were told that without choice they were being recruited to fight the war against oppression. Two of the students and one gunman went to collect the blankets and clothes from the domes. Whilst they were gone a chilling order came from the leader in a husky forceful "Hey Gondo shot these three and the rest start moving." Gondo who looked so ruthless stepped forward and asked the three to kneel down. Garikayi who was standing a few yards from the leader threw himself under his feet begging for the three men to be spared. "Sir, these men have been so good to us, they are not evil, it is because of them that we have had the chance read and write and most of their fellow whites don't like them because of that, plea . . . ." Shut up before I shoot you too" Gondo interrupted him with a shove. All students moved forward and stood by their headmaster and the two teachers and in one voice said "you shoot them, you shoot us" That went down in history because the three men were spared but the students were taken including Garikayi. To give the group a head start the two gunmen stayed at the school holding everyone hostage for two days and on the third day they vanished during the night. It was almost noon the following day that everyone began to realize that they were safe and that the gunmen were gone. Shungu was devastated at the loss of his brother, in his mind he thought he would never see him again and that made him feel very alone because his brother was the only family he knew. One thing that made him proud was to know that it was through Garikayi that the headmaster's life was spared.

Two weeks later, the Mission school was declared unsafe and was shut down. Shungu had no alternative but to return to the orphanage. Father James welcomed him with open arms. Since his brother was abducted he never dropped a tear because he kept thinking he would see his brother back safe and sound. When he started explaining about the incident to Father James he broke down and cried uncontrollably and as much as Father James tried to comfort him, he just could not stop. Father James decided to leave him for a while because it seemed all the pain and loss that he had suffered had come down at that moment. He was quiet and very reserved for days that followed. Father James decided to give Shungu a job to keep him busy, hoping that would help him to forget his pain. Shungu then 16 years old became a much-deserved hand at the Orphanage – preparing meals for the orphans and being a general hand whenever his skills were required. At the age of 18, Father James taught him how to drive a tractor, which they used to plough the fields for the Orphanage. Once in a while when the Orphanage's tractor driver was on call in different lines of duty, Shungu would fill in to work the earth on the not so large plot.

One wet Sunday morning after the Orphanage's traditional church services. Shungu was sermonized to Father James's humble quarters for what he thought to be a briefing, but to his shock, Father James had found him a job. He was to become a tractor driver for a farm owner he not only knew so well, but loathed immensely too – Stewart. Father James told him that Stewart, who had aged considerably, sought a young obedient driver to work under the direct supervision of one of his sons Sidney; who had now assumed the role of Farm Manager, grooming to become owner. The position had risen after Forogo Parafini; former driver had been dismissed on account of old age. The good Father had told Shungu all this unaware of the fact that he knew the farm so well; well enough to remember not only the ruthless killing of his parents, but the lashes on his behind as well. When the name was mentioned to him, Shungu instantly saw two names flash through his mind – Spinach and Stewart, these were names that not even the most severe concussion could erase from his mind. At first he was scared Spinach would recognize him and start the alarm bells. He knew that Father James was not asking him but was ordering him and so had no choice but to go. The suffering he endured at the Seven Stud during his childhood flashed before him, he looked worried and scared. Father James noticed his hesitation to the proposal and quickly chipped in (thinking he was worried about leaving the orphanage:

"Don't worry about us we will be fine. You must count yourself lucky that you are going to this farm under the supervision of Stewart's son, if you had been summoned a few years back when Stewart was in control then and only then would you have had need to worry because he was the most ruthless man to walk the earth."

"I couldn't agree more" Shungu said without thought.

"Do you know Stewart?" Father James asked with a surprise look on his face.

"No . . . no, I just remembered a story I heard from one of the students at school" he lied. This bit of information about some changes at the farm made him relax a bit and for Father James's sake showed enthusiasm for the job offer.

CHAPTER THREE

S IDNEY HAMILTON TOOK an instant liking for the English speaking, energetic and smartly dressed Shungu. After the hurried introductions, Father James who had driven Shungu over left, for he had urgent business to attend to. Shungu was quick to observe that Stewart's son though very much like his fathers feature-wise, the younger Stewart had a human heart inside him contrasting with the one made of rock in his father. He also observed that the farm atmosphere had acquired a new tone – that of lax; as if a menacing evil and dark cloud that had been the farm trademarks, had been removed. Shungu could not help wondering where Stewart was, but he knew he was around somewhere even though he had not seen him. However, the slavery and toil still existed, this he saw for himself as they drove through the fields in Father James's car to the farm mansion. He also knew that Spinach was very much alive because he was the one that gave them directions to the Hamilton Mansion. He had developed Grey hair and looked done in by age and a crippled conscience owing to the countless deaths he had been directly responsible for but he still looked as fit as a bull. What pleased Shungu most was the fact that Spinach showed not one flicker of recognition when their eyes met.

Sidney took Shungu on a familiarization tour of the farm in a pick-up truck that had known better days. He remembered the truck as the one that Stewart used to romp around in during those gone by days. Shungu did not give any hint of the fact that he knew the farm well enough except for some rather massive developments. The compound huts had been re-thatched and generally looked healthy – thanks to Sidney. The once dusty roads had been tarred, cotton fields stretching endlessly, and a lot more than Shungu cared to stress. After the tour Sidney drove Shungu to the Garage where farm equipment was stored. Parked inside the shed was a 45 hoarse powered Marcy Ferguson tractor that had had a complete engine overhaul. Shungu loved the feel of the metal that had a bright red shine to it, unlike the old beat-up tractor at the orphanage that had to be repaired more times than the hours spent tilting the land. Sidney explained to Shungu about his duties on the farm and that it was his responsibility to see that the tractor was in good condition and well maintained. He also told him that he would report to no other person than himself (Sidney). That was good news to Shungu because that eliminated Spinach as his foreman. The two climbed back into the truck and drove back to the mansion. During the drive Sidney was saying:

"Of course it's going to be hard work, but you will get a handsome package to come with it. Dad suggested I organize accommodation for you at the compound where every other black worker lives, but I feel I should do something better for you. We've got a nice little chalet built on a cleft not far from the housemaid's quarters. It was initially built for purposes of summer recoils but ever since our rooms got ventilators installed it became void so I feel you should use it."

"Thank you so much sir, I appreciate your kindness and I promise to do my duties to your satisfaction. Does the housemaid stay all by herself? Shungu quipped, completed relaxed."

"Now don't run out and get bright ideas, she is a widowed forty seven years old, far too old for a handsome young man like you. We decided that she stays close to the main house – away from the compound because she also does our cooking and Dad being so unpopular with the workforce thought she might be persuaded to poison our food – it was just a security measure – come on, I'll show you the chalet!" Sidney explained.

***

After Sidney had gone, Shungu sank onto the bed. It was a clean and cozy little place that included a double bed, wardrobe, kitchen unit and sink within its confines. Shungu could not believe his luck; he could not believe that this was the same farm he had grown to fear when he was a child, but somehow he was not surprised because he believed his parents where guiding him and probably that explained all the occurrences. He immediately remembered his father's last words 'stop those devils . . .', and stop them Shungu had vowed to do which meant killing Spinach and Stewart, that was why his ancestors had led him back to the farm. However, he resolved to killing Stewart in a manner that would leave him suspect free because he had taken a liking for Stewart's son Sidney and did not want to end this new found friendship on a tragic note. He sensed that Sidney, though a cool and lovable character – also had a vipers capabilities on the flipside of his nature, and for him to discover that Shungu had murdered his father, would lead to the revelation of what he was made of – the suppressed components of his father in him were sure to boil, and surface within moments of such a discovery. The best scheme was to strike clandestinely, then shift suspicion and evidence to someone else that would then be on the receiving end of Sidney's wrath. Shungu already had a candidate for this end – SPINARCH. This was sure to be the best vengeance he could ever give for the loathsome foreman.

Sidney had instructed Shungu to relax for the entire afternoon, and then start work on a tobacco field extension first thing the following day. So he decided to go for a walk. He locked up his chalet, descended the wooded stairs to a cobble stone walkway, and then turned left to a footpath leading to the compound. To get to the compound from the chalet, he had to circle almost seven acres covering the sorghum field but since he was in no hurry, decided it was no sweat. Passing through the sorghum field, he watched in awe as women and men labored in sweet silence, most of them paused to stare at the stranger clad in a bell bottom trouser, balloon sleeved shirt and canvas shoes (all donated to the orphanage from Germany). The stare made Shungu uneasy but he kept up his pace as if the eyes boring into his flesh were part of the wind blowing. Approaching the end of the field he slowed down as reality downed on him that an elderly slim woman, a short distance yonder, was closely eyeing him as he approached and as he got closer the woman still gazed at him – this time with wide-eyed wonder. The look on her face was beginning to send shivers down his spine. Suddenly the woman laid down her hoe and seated herself on the recently weeded soil that bore the sorghum crop and began to cry. It began as a soft whimper and culminated in an unrestrained vocal haul – it was pitiful and Shungu was forced to stop. None of her fellow workers dared come to investigate for fear of what could happen to them if the foreman suddenly materialized and found them unemployed. Deep down they feared for her because she was sitting on crops, her husband who was slaving a few yards away dashed towards her. All this happened while Shungu just stood there drained out of words. When the husband reached her, he halted breathlessly and bent over: "Amai Nhau (Nhau's mother) what is wrong?" He asked dropping to his knees and holding her by the shoulders and shaking her gently:
"The boy" screamed Amai Nhau pointing at Shungu. Baba Nhau (Nhau's father) swung his gaze at Shungu and froze for a second then after a moment he stammered at the boy:
"R . . . . R . . . Rutendo? . . . R . . ?" – It was Shungu's turn to freeze . . .
"Is . . . it rea . . . lly you?" he mumbled. Shungu tried to say something but nothing came out. The man whispered in his wife's ear and whatever he said got

her shooting onto her feet and drying her eyes. The husband then stepped closer to the boy and darting quick sideways glances whispered:

"Rutendo, if you are the new tractor driver – Good – I know this is all puzzling to you but I'll explain later. Come to the compound tonight when its dark and I'll tell you the whole story, don't be afraid we mean well".

That was all that was said and the couple was sooner engrossed in their toil as if nothing had happened. Shungu still confused made a U-turn and headed back to the chalet.

The routine at he compound after working hours was as it had always been when Shungu and his family lived there. ALIVE! Men could be seen sprawled exhaustedly on reed mats besides the fire on which their evening meals would be cooking. Some would be in huts sharing home brewed beer and discussing their various cultures and traditions for none of them dared discuss politics – religions? Yes, but never the boss or such related issues. Children could be heard humming on tuneless songs while waiting for that much deserved meal – sadza and beans. Mothers were a rare sight for they would be indoors preparing meals and doing the usual domestic cores that would have accumulated due to lack of time to sort them out.

It was already dark when Shungu arrived at the compound. He made it seem as if he was out on a casual meet the people tour because he knew Spinach would be about the place in his usual quest for negative small talk. Shungu did not go deep into the compound because suddenly one rough hand grabbed hold of his wrist and lead him back into the sorghum field. He was about to resist when he realized it was the same old man he had come to see so he followed behind and after what looked like ten minutes or so he was led into a grass thatched kitchen hut whose confines was the thin old woman Amai Nhau. She was alone and bending over a large three-legged pot which was on the fire and coming from it was the soothing aroma of sweet potatoes. Once inside, Baba Nhau kicked the wooden door shut and bolted up before waving Shungu onto a fire side stool. He peeped through the triangle shaped window to make sure there were no eve droppers then he wedged in a card board box to seal off as well as keep the pending discussion within the hut. His wife had settled down on a goat skin mat and was watching Shungu closely, sizing him up. Baba Nhau came forward and sat opposite Shungu on a huge stone and began:

"My son; this indeed is a typical example of Gods miracles. Do you remember us? Of course you don't – that woman over there (pointing to the wife) is your Aunt Matilda, Last of the children in your mother's family. I'm sure you remember her, she always loved to carry you on her back when you were a toddler". Shungu's face brightened – he had remembered his Aunt very well. Looking at her now in the faint glow of firelight, the memories began to flood back. She had been a very stout woman those days, and looked much changed now that she'd lost a lot of weight. Shungu stood up suddenly, nestled beside his Aunt on the goat skin mat and she began to sob again as he put his arms around her tenderly:

"Oh Aunt . . . . I remember now . . . . my sweet Aunt", he whispered almost choking with emotion. Somewhere, his Uncle's voice continued to filter:

"We could never have forgotten you son even if you had come back 40 years later – here, come and sit on the stool and lets have a man to man talk – let the poor woman sob herself dry, she needs time to recover from the shock, it certainly is a shock because we heard that the whole family was gunned down – If it was not for that wide fore-head of your father's feature I would never have recognized you." Shungu pulled away from his Aunt and sprang back onto the stool. He was overcome by a deep-sited joy to be reunited with blood relatives.

"Tell me something, where you the only survivor?" came baba Nhau.

"Oh no! Kuda also survived but he was abducted by Freedom Fighters and I have not heard from him since, so I don't know whether he's alive or dead." Shungu said sadly and went on to tell them the story from the day they left the compound to-date and the reason why they both had changed their names. The old couple listened intently amazement vivid on their faces as he spoke. After the final episode, Baba Nhau sucked in a lung full of air then exhaled noisily:

"Very intriguing, my son, your ancestors are definitely guiding you and I just hope your brother is still alive. Here things have improved slightly except for Spinach of course he's still a pain in the crotch but small boss Sidney is not too hungry for his gossip so he jumps that gradient and goes straight to Stewart with his nasty reports. Stewart then orders his son to act. Stewart has not been seen around lately – rumor has it that he has a terminal illness and is bed ridden but even then one can't be too careful.

"I am so glad to see you my son, you are the only one left to remind me of my mother's child – poor kid she was so full of life, so strong and for her to die like a . . ." Amai Nhau said more to herself (about her sister) and began to weep again.

"Amai Nhau please! It's been years! This Aunt of yours must have a lake of tears in that head of hers – since the death of her sister she's been raining tears at the mare thought of that incident, but now that you are here, surely that is suppose to make life better" Uncle said and went on changing the subject:

"Do you remember our Son Nhau who used to play with Kuda? He just vanished one night without word; them later we heard he had left a message with his girlfriend that he was going to join the armed struggle. It's been six years now and we have not heard from him; another thought that makes your Aunt flood.

"Oh yeah! I remember he used to make mud cars for me and my friends." Shungu said laughing. Baba Nhau still had questions to ask:

"Tell me will you be staying here in the compound?"

"No! Sidney set me up in a nice little chalet near the main house. He looks like a good man to me. What do you think?" Shungu asked his Uncle who replied:

Very nice he is, but do not get too warm headed – remember a baby snake no matter how small is still a snake, its venom might even be double lethal than the parent – just play safe". Mai Nhau uncoiled from the goat skin mat and fetched two wooden plates from a unit made of mud and polished by dung. Lifting off the heavy lid from the steaming pot, she dished out portions of sweet potatoes and served them to the two men. While they ate, their discussion drove from farm current affairs to religion and politics then finally leveled on the hot issue of vengeance. Baba Nhau went on to tell him how one day his Aunt had bravely captured a live mature back mamba in a snare sack and how she had attempted to smuggle it into Spinach's quarters for it to attack him once he walked into his bedroom and how the attempt was foiled by one of Spinach's children who had suddenly materialized from hell knows where and she had managed to dive behind a thicket unnoticed by the child. The mission was aborted and the snake was killed. Shungu was thoroughly thrilled by the story such that he gave his Aunt a look of admiration. He now knew he had someone to help him in his murder plot when due.

Baba Nhau heaved himself up from the stool and strode over to the window; removed the cardboard he had wedged in it and peeped into the dark night – satisfied there was no one about he turned to look at Shungu and said:

"I'm sure we had a private meeting in here – no Spinach fears, I suggest you run along son. Catch some rest and tomorrow I want you to go about your duties like it's the first time you've been here. I know the safest places and times to get in touch with you so leave the contacts to me". Shungu thanked and gave them both a hug and saw himself out of the hut and like a ghost slid into the night.

⚜

Shungu loved the sound of the Ferguson as he raved and raved the engine while looking at the unending stretch of uncultivated land before him. It was a cloudy morning with occasional breaks of sunlight; a sign of a possible rainfall but Shungu resolved to upturn two or three hectares before lunch break. He shifted his gears into forward and let the disk harrow down. The tractor jerked forward the huge hind tires domineering over miniature vegetation as they spun forward. He glanced over his shoulder to watch as the metal disks chewed through earth leaving a streak of freshly dug earth behind and the reassuring sweet smell of ploughed field. Shungu did twenty seven laps making close knit U-turns after one and a half miles stretches before he brought the machine to a halt and turned off the engine to give the pistons a well deserved break and dismounted. He looked at the job he had done and nodded to himself with satisfaction. Sidney drove-by to see the newly hired man's progress and was impressed with the results that he smiled and gave Shungu the thumb-up, before driving off.

Getting ready to mount on the tractor, Shungu caught a glimpse of a man perched against a mahogany tree not far from the tractor. A second and through look revealed the man to be none other than Spinach with his beady eyes fixed on Shungu, watching every move mischievously. Shungu felt a rapid flow of revulsion at the sight of the man. A demonic surge of fury compounded by a savage and long-standing animosity made him take steps towards Spinach, but he quickly realized it was not the time and place and that he did not want to attract attention on himself; with difficulty he controlled himself and without a word flung himself on to the tractor seat. That did not seem to please Spinach at all because he expected some sort of salute or rather some kind of knee bending like the rest of the peasants did when they saw him:

"Hey you!" Spinach shouted with an authority-ridden voice. Shungu turned slowly and looked directly at Spinach but did not say a word.

"You don't just turn off the tractor engine when it pleases you. I have orders to see to it that this stretch of land is ready for planting by tomorrow. That Tobacco crop over there should not be too distant in age to the one we intend to plant on this piece of land. So you'd better damn well keep those disks busy until and only until I tell you to break off be it for tea or lunch. For your information I am the foreman around here – MANAGER! to be precise" Spinach shouted spitting in the process. Shungu eyed him sizzling with rage, for a moment then turning the ignition keys he replied with an edge to his voice:

"If the boss wanted me to know I had a supervisor, he'd have introduced you to me but he didn't so if you'll excuse me. I've got work to do". Spinach felt his temper rise because throughout his work life on the farm no one had ever spoken to him like that, not even the retired tractor driver:

"Now you listen to me young man and listen well, I've been on this farm for . . ." Spinach was about to say something but Shungu did not wait for him to finish his statement, instead he shifted his gears and shot into motion leaving Spinach panting with anger:

"Your days are numbered on this farm boy! You've just crossed swords with evil" Spinach shouted, but he could have been shouting to himself because Shungu was already yards away and with the deafening sound of the tractor his threat was his own. End of day, tired and mud caked, Shungu drove the tractor into its bay and made for the chalet. He did not encounter Spinach again that day and as tired as he was it was for the best. When he got back to the Chalet he was surprised to find that the maid had left him some dinner by the door step. That night he slept like a log.

Sunday was usually a relaxing day at the Seven Stud because the peasants were now being let off work at 12.00 noon and everyone would be free to do what they so wished except leave the farm. Shungu who by then had been on the farm for nearly a month had got quite accustomed to the environment of the Stud and was sitting in his chalet thinking of how he was going to spend the Sunday afternoon. 'Stewart' came to his mind but he though against it since Baba Nhau had asked him to wait in case they connected the new arrival with a mysterious death. He decided to take a stroll to the compound tuck shop hoping to meet his uncle or aunt whom he had not seen or heard from since the last meeting. When he got to the tuck shop he bought some fresh milk served in a gourd and loitered around sipping milk with his eyes roving in hope of taking a glimpse of his new found and only living relatives. He did not want to ask anyone in case people got suspicious, but to no avail. On his way back, he almost brushed past a girl of about 17 who seemed totally immersed in hunting for something in the grass bordering the footpath from the tuck-shop. When she looked up at him and moved to give him way Shungu grinded himself to a halt, looking at her his heart lurch inside him. Despite the pathetic clothes she wore, the girl was well bathed. She had a long innocent face on which stuck out a small almost flattish nose, a proportionally sized mouth and two large eyes that looked deeply worried. She had a light chocolate color complexion, her hair cut short fitting perfectly on the rather small round head. Her breasts, covered by a thin film of the fabric of her worn out blouse were firm and full with the nipples almost piercing through. She was tall and slim with her bust seeming to shrink about the waist and then suddenly bulging out into shapely hips giving her the most breath-taking curves Shungu had ever seen. By all means the girl was beautiful, so beautiful that Shungu seemed to have been hypotenuse:

"Do you intend to pass or not?" the girl asked with a voice that sounded like music in Shungu's ears and bringing him back to earth.

"Oh eer yea – I am passing; ee . . . e . . . r have you lost something?" he asked eyeing her closely.

"Yes I have – my mother gave me a pound to buy some corn meal . . . and . . . I . . . I dropped it somewhere along this path" she replied still searching frantically.

"Maybe someone picked it up", Shungu suggested making her panic even more.

"Oh I hope not because my mother will skin me alive – it's the last money she had between now and the next pay day" she explained still searching.

"This is a busy path and I think chances of finding the money are very slim, don't you have your own saving to re . . . ." Shungu chipped in trying to help and making matters worse.

"Look! If I did I would not be bothering myself would I. Besides who are you to put me under cross-examination. Please be on your way and let me get on with my problem" she said her voice rising and looking straight into his eyes.

"ee . . . er . . . I'm only trying to help, will you accept a pound from me? . . . . ee . . . eeh you can give me back when you get paid" Shungu said genuinely. She looked at him, the big eyes uncertain, then she let them drop shyly to her bare feet. Shungu noticed her reluctant and confused innocence of being torn between a stranger and an angry mother:

"I'm sure you have seen me around, my name is Shungu and I am the tractor driver. I won't mention to anyone that I gave you the pound, you can just give it back when you get your wage" he said stretching his only pound; a sacrifice he was willing to endure for this beautiful girl's sake. She took it hesitantly.

"Thank you very much . . . . I'll pay you back . . . my . . . my name is Sarah and my job is to feed chickens and pick eggs – I must run now" She explained and bustled off before he could say another word. Shungu stood there watching her as she gracefully trotted away. She turned round, smiled and hurriedly continued in her flurry. Shungu smiled back and began his journey back to the chalet. He felt twenty times larger than life; 'she's a master piece' he thought to himself as he added a spring to his strides. He pulled his one shilling left in his pocket and wondered what he was going to do until pay day which was three week away then quickly brushed the thought aside because he felt that nothing could beat the fact that he gave to the most beautiful girl and the fact that since she said she would pay back that meant he would see her again. The thought brought a tingle of excitement so much that the distance to his chalet seemed like a very short walk because his mind was filled with nothing other than the face of Sarah. On nearing the chalet all thoughts of Sarah vanished from his mind when he saw Sidney standing by his doorstep with Spinach. They were watching him as he approached. Composing himself he strode closer as if unperturbed. It was Sidney who spoke first.

"Shungu I've been waiting for you!"

"Something the matter Sir" he asked puzzled.

"Nothing serious. I've just been to the patch you' ploughed and I must say I'm pleased with what you've done." He said and went on: "but . . . er the farm foreman here . . . (Pointing at Spinach) says on numerous occasions he has asked you to go easy on the tractor lest it develops a tumor in the engine and you told him that the bosses, and he (Spinach) should jump into the lake and drown because you are your own boss; is that true?" Shungu was not at all surprised because he knew Spinach could never report anything accurately without exaggeration, for a moment he did not speak as he looked sternly at Spinach who was wearing a face ridden with mischief, then he turned to Sidney and replied:

"Sir all I can say is that the man is lying right through his teeth." Spinach as if suddenly switched on to a high voltage plug, sprung forward as if to attack:

"Are you calling me a liar haa? Boss Sidney knows I've never told one li . . . ."

"Damn it Spinach! Hold your horses" Sidney screamed ready to snap. "I'm talking to Shungu; your turn to speak will be announced – jeepers!" He added shaking his head.

"Sir; this man might say what he feels fit but as long as my conscience is clear, I will not move a hair. He's lying. Since I started working here, he's been bothering me about violating the farm rules by giving the engine some air, saying I could only stop to breath for 30 minutes when he tells me to do so since he was the farm manager. That in its self made me realize that he knew nothing about the tractor and so I ignored him and kept giving the tractor a break whenever I felt the engine heating up. I also told him that I will wait for a formal introduction from the boss before taking any orders from him". Shungu explained suppressing his anger. Sidney was intelligent enough to know the truth and a lie, he frowned turning to Spinach:

"Spinach! You've worked on this farm for years and you saw me grow up, I'd hate to box your face and I've had enough of you running to my father and telling him all kind of boloney. From now on you report to me. I don't want to hear dad telling me to investigate on any rubbish you'll have told him. I am your boss now not dad. Shungu sounds genuine and I believe every word he said, besides, I am happy with what he has done so far. Now listen and listen well – I want you to program what I'm about to say into that white staff you've got upstairs you call a brain. Shungu works only on my orders *not* yours or dad's. He reports to me and only me. Don't ever, EVER! Go interfering with his duties. Do I make myself clear?" Sidney asked almost shouting.

"Yes Boss" Spinach whispered looking like an in-law caught stealing food in the kitchen – embarrassed. He shuffled off without looking back. Sidney watched him and swore under his breath:

"You know what, that idiot is always stirring trouble for other workers just because he's dad's close trouble shooter and he now thinks he owns the farm. It's about time he was put back in his rightful place – The farm worker not owner. I'm sorry Shungu I knew all along that he had made up the sordid tale. He doesn't like anyone who looks threatening to his job so just ignore him and do your job because he's not going to sneak all over you again – he got the message." Sidney assured Shungu.

"Thank you, sir. By the way I completed the task you gave me and need to know the next assignment". Shungu said grinning. Sidney had been scrutinizing Shungu with an expression on his face that he failed to place. There was a distinct glow in his eyes that was not far from a deep concealed desire. As if suddenly waking up from a dream, Sidney stammered:

"er . . . . Yes . . . . Yes . . . Well, . . . er we've got another patch of land that needs plowing for our cornflower, but its not as vast as what you worked on today, I'll show you tomorrow . . . er . . . Father James tells me you received some basic training in technical skills – can you fix cars?".

"I have some knowledge but I mastered skills in plumbing and general repair work" Shungu replied.

"In that case you'll be much more than a tractor driver. I have a combine harvester that needs fixing. Once you start on it I will add two pounds to your current wages per week – would you like that?" Sidney offered smiling. Shungu gulped; the money was far much more than he'd anticipated. That was almost a farm manager's salary.

"Oh yes oooh yes! Sir. Thank you, thank you boss!" Shungu exclaimed excitedly almost wanting to hug hin.

"I spoke to my father at length over the issue and it was a hustle convincing him because the wages are higher, much higher than the foreman but I feel you deserve better. You're an asset around here . . . . and . . . . I . . . . er . . . . oh forget it, I'll see you tomorrow" Sidney said chewing some of the words and slowly walking away.

Shungu was left standing outside his chalet, a puzzled expression on his face. Somehow he could not quite figure all this kindness from the young boss. The way he softened down when he spoke to him. The weird looks in his eyes. There was something about him that Shungu desperately wanted to explore, to dig deep and discover. One thing he knew for certain was that Sidney liked him immensely – 'Why?' Shungu did not have the faintest idea. As he unlocked his door, all thoughts of Sidney disappeared and where replaced by those of Sarah. The mental image pictures brought the girl in bright focus. He imagined her dressed in a tight fitting skirt and a flared blouse. How completely irresistible she looked. He did not want to fool himself into thinking the thoughts about Sarah were nothing but a passing flight of fancy. Shungu knew he wanted her for himself. The question was how to find her and talk to her again without raising any alarm especially with the eagle eye of Spinach because without question Spinach would have something nasty to say to Sarah's parents. Another thought hit him, 'maybe she is already married off to some guy and just waiting for the dowry to be paid' the thought brought cold sweats on his forehead – there were so many what ifs that he did not remember what time he finally slept chewing on the Sarah bone.

CHAPTER FOUR

IN A ROOM that passed for a Lounge, Spinach was sitting on a stool leaning over a plate of his special meal of Sadza (made of white corn meal) and dried fish mixed with vegetables. His face appeared old and weather beaten in the glow of the lamplight. Opposite him was his frail looking wife busy knitting and listening quietly to what the husband was saying:

"That boy has really gone too far. He'll be lucky to last another week on this farm." Spinach said, swallowing a chunk of fish he'd been chewing.

"What has he done to you? Baba Sarah sometimes you go over board with your wickedness. I've watched silently as you brought untold misery to countless families all because of greed and hunger for power. One day – cross ooh! – you will pay dearly for your evil ways." The wife pointed out licking her fingers and swishing them over her face in a swear gesture.

"Shut your mouth woman! You have me to thank for living in a three-roomed house and wearing nice clothes. It's all because I work hard and my boss knows it. You'd be out in the cold like all the other farm dogs if I didn't protect the boss!" Spinach shouted poking the wife on her forehead.

"What nice clothes? Our daughter is a moving joke dressed the way she does in rags and you have the nerve to talk about nice clothes. The daughter of Chikonzo next door dresses far better than Sarah, and yet Chikonzo earns much less than you!" The wife retaliated with a chuckle.

"That is your job not mine, if we had a son, I'd make sure he was well clothed. Daughters are their mother's responsibility. Talk about that idiot Chikonzo, he togs up his daughter because he wants her to win the heart of Bobo so that he can claim dowry. Such thoughts, I don't entertain." He said with a sneer.

"At least he cares about his daughter's welfare, but you feel having a girl is nothing but troubles. Do you remember that even for Sarah to have attended Sub A, we had to fight? Yet, since she started working you've been taking her wages and leaving her with a few pennies – you make your own child slave for nothing. If it wasn't for the fact that she has nowhere to go, she could have long since stopped working and most probably run aw . . . ." Spinach's wife complained almost in tears.

"Hey . . . Hey . . ." Spinach broke in . . . . "You are talking too much. Are these the conversations you have with your daughter in my absence . . . hmmm? Why don't you talk to Bobo when next he comes with his delivery for the tuck shop to take your daughter away if you think she's not happy here hmmmm . . . . He said throwing his arms around. The wife rose without a word and started clearing the dishes from the improvised table. Spinach belched loudly patting his belly and called out:

"Sarah!" Sarah, who had been having her supper in the kitchen, listening intently to her parent's discussion, rose promptly and strode into the living room wiping her face with the palm of her hand with suppressed exasperation. She stood by the door without a word waiting for his father to say why he had called her:

"Whose manner-less child is this that comes and stands before me without respect? Is this what your mother teaches you? – Brat! Kneel down before I turn you into minced meat." Spinach screamed charging towards his daughter. The wife intercepted clapping her hands and on bended knees – Museyamwa, mhofu yem'kono, zenda nechikaka, mutunhu une mago – chokwadi mwana akanganisa, chimuregererayi ndapota shewe (praising his totem and asking for forgiveness on her daughter's behalf). Spinach suddenly turned round and went back to his stool pushing his wife aside in the process. Sarah who had sat down was suppressing tears that were threatening to pour out.

"You stand before me again and that will be the day you walk out of here and never to come back – do you hear me? Is that what you were taught at that stupid school you were going to haaaah? Your mother was accusing me of taking all your money; did you not show her the five pennies that I gave you two weeks ago from your wages hmmm? Sarah was about to answer but Spinach went on without giving room for answers until the wife cut in:

"How do you expect Sarah to answer any of your questions when you just keep asking non-stop, besides, what dress do you expect Sarah to buy with five pennies. My wages, you insist I use to buy grocery, Sarah's and yours; you blow up in the compound tavern entertaining your whores. My silence does not mean I'm dumb, it's just that I fear you could turn your boss on me."

"Don't interrupt me when I'm talking woman! I am getting impatient with you shooting your mouth as if you're talking to this silly girl of yours – remember I am the head of this house. Compound Tavern! Do you realize that all the drunks in the Tavern compete with each other buying me booze because they all seek favors from me? They want my protection and occupational security. I don't spend a dime on any of those cheap, half-naked, cow dung clunking imitations of humanity that mob the tavern. I am a big man in these parts, so don't you just shoot your mouth away based on rumor most probably from this brat of yours!" Spinach said sarcastically and pompously.

"You really amaze me; When its pay day, Sarah is your daughter because you want her money but today she's a brat and my child not yours . . . aah . . . yah! One thing you seem to have forgotten too is the fact that you are no different from those people you are calling names. Being a foreman does not mean you are no longer a black African. They may be poor, but they need to be respected and be treated like humans not animals. Don't cheat yourself and say they respect you because they don't – all they do is fear you which mean given the chance they will turn you into minced meat. Right now, I don't even have friends because the women think I am a traitor like you, I . . . ." Spinach's wife said in a rasp voice. Sarah smoothly left the room as the argument escalated. She only prayed it did not drag into a punch up. Ever since she was knee high, she'd been audience to many fights between her parents usually ending up with her mother nursing cuts and bruises. She went into her parent's bedroom where she kept her worn out blankets and brought them to the kitchen where she slept. She spread them on the floor and tucked herself in with most of the body exposed through the holes on the blankets. The sooner she put her head down; the suppressed tears started flowing down her cheeks. Crying herself to sleep was part of her life, but, this night seemed to be different. The thought of the young man that helped her with a pound wiped away all the tears. Sarah felt an excitement she could not understand – 'Shungu is so kind hearted and so han . . . . oh forget it' she thought, with these wonderful thoughts in her mind, she drifted off to wonderland – a land of dreams and in that dream was Shungu!

Basikoro who came to tell the foreman that he was about to close the tuck-shop and needed him to count and collect the day-takings interrupted the heated argument between Spinach and his wife. By the time Spinach came back, the wife was in bed pretending to be fast asleep. Her mind was focused on her daughter and what was to become of her. She knew young men in the compound were avoiding Sarah because of the father's cruelty. 'Maybe if I talk to Bobo he can get her a job as a Maid in the high density suburb where he lives' she thought quietly. That thought pleased her even though she knew she had to be very tactful because if it got to Spinach's ears she'd be as good as dead. Bobo was only coming two weeks from that day which meant she still had time to plan how to go about it. Turning on her side and giving Spinach her back, she closed her eyes and her thoughts.

Shungu kept himself buried in his work for the next five days that followed; he was even asked to deliver over 500 egg trays to the town center. He was generally liked by many at the farm for his politeness, kindness and cheerfulness. Most even hoped he would be promoted to the rank of a foreman and replace the hateful

Spinach. While Shungu basked in the glory of Sidney's intense love, Spinach on the other hand, was seething with jealous coupled with chronic hatred. On many occasions, Spinach had watched from a distance, Shungu and Sidney laughing in a clear gesture of true friendship. The two, boss and employee had almost become inseparable. At odd times in the night, Sidney would call on Shungu at his chalet. Sometimes bring with him food from the Mansion and share it with Shungu. What surprised Shungu though was Sidney's behavior sometimes on these night calls, he'd swindle next to him, too close for comfort and begin to fondle him playfully – not to mention the kiss on the check when he left. Shungu innocently thought that was how white people showed brotherly love, but deep down, he knew that something sinister was behind Sidney's overtly peculiar fondness. Not wanting to jump to conclusions he decided to wait and see what happens even though these night visits disrupted his plans to visit his Uncle and Aunt to discuss the final plot to avenge his murdered family.

A few times after work, Shungu would roam around the tuck-shop in the hope that he would bump into Sarah, but all he saw were old ladies and grumpy old men. The following Sunday, which was two days away, he vowed he would look for Sarah until he found her. It was to be a special day for everyone on the Farm because a dancing group from another compound was coming to perform – an event that amazed everyone when it was announced by Spinach through Sidney's directive. Laborers could not stop talking about such a change nor could they stop wondering what a good man the young boss was. When Sidney came to see him that evening Shungu politely told him that he would be very busy with his laundry and general clean up of the chalet throughout Saturday and Sunday to which Sidney gladly agreed, reason being he was taking his father (Stewart) to visit his sister in Harare and would only be back on Wednesday the following week. He went on to say that was the reason he arranged a joyous day for his workers because his father would be away. This was good news for Shungu. This meant he had four full days to himself and maybe Sarah. He had to put a lot of effort to hide his excitement.

Knowing that the boss was away, Shungu decided to sleep in an extra three hours, in a way it wouldn't have made any difference because it was his day off but each time he tried to sleep in Sidney would make his unusual drop ins. When he finally got up, he gathered his laundry (mainly uniforms) and using a home-made bar of soap given to him by the house-maid, busied himself with the hand washing, rinsed and neatly hung the clothes along the hedge that divided the chalet and the golf course. Locking up the chalet, he decided to walk over to the compound ground were the workers were about to be entertained by the Traditional Dancers. Passing through a sugar-cane plantation, he helped himself to one and that was enough to shorten the distance to the compound's open ground.

There was a crowd of people surrounding the small dusty ground when Shungu arrived. He glanced around the crowd as the sound of drums picked up beat. He knew Sarah was somewhere in the crowd because when he passed the compound it was totally deserted except for the chickens. Suddenly he caught a glimpse of her on the other section of the ground, her tall frame visible above the heads of the crowd. From where he was standing, Shungu was sure she had seen him. Sarah had indeed seen him and felt a wave of excitement. She was clad in her usual faded oversized dress that had, had its fair share of use with sandals made from animal hide and rubber. Her hair was in neat plaits that her friend had plaited bringing out that natural beauty that had knocked Shungu off the ground and landed head over heal. A friend standing next to Sarah did not miss the reaction and excitement on Sarah's face when she saw Shungu, but could not understand why . . .

"What is so exciting? The dancers are just getting ready to start but you seem to be flying all of a sudden" she asked puzzled about the sudden change.

"Nothing! Just enjoying my day off – hey look!" Sarah exclaimed pointing at the Gure dancer that had now taken the floor. Her friend (Shamiso) swung round to look. This Sarah had done purposely to divert her friend's attention. A quick glance towards where Shungu had been standing revealed a blank space – he was no longer there. Her friend not easily fooled let her eyes follow:

"Who on earth are you spying on?" the friend asked.

"Nobody! Why the interest?" Sarah replied as she scanned the crowd almost in a desperate manner.

"Oh it's no big deal; it's just that you took extra care with your dressing today as if you expected to bump into someone rather special". Shamiso said laughing. Sarah turned to look at the rather attractive girl by her side dressed in a simple cotton dress; annoyance cloning her next wore.

"You always love to see me dressed in rugs don't you?" she asked irritated.

"No . . . . no . . . Sarah . . . but I am your best friend we are suppose to share secrets". The girl tried to explain. On the other hand, Shungu having spotted Sarah, circled the ground through the throng towards the section he had seen her and by mixing with the people, Shungu hoped to recapture the feeling of belonging but too much time had past, too many lives had changed and it was only natural that his life too had changed. It must have been Sidney who made all these changes but each time he thought of Sidney his mind would jolt with red flags and he could not understand why. Shungu's gaze scanned the rowdy immature slightly intoxicated young gure dancers thundering away in the middle of the crowd-made circle to the rhythm of drumbeats, then moved to the girls cheering on the sidelines. As his eyes swept over the somewhat overjoyed girls, they rested briefly on Sarah, continued to her friend then came back to her. She stood mesmerized, eyes locked with a silent message that could not be denied – they were in love. In that instant they both realized they felt more than just friendship. Shungu moved closer to her:

"Hello Sarah" He said, not caring who saw or heard him, it was like no one else existed.

"Hello eeh . . . Shh . . . Shungu" Sarah mumbled. She too was far from perturbed by who ever else were about.

"Like to take a walk?" He inquired searching her face.

"Eeh . . . . Yee . . . ah, but my parents are here somewhere and if they see us together I'll be in deep trouble" Sarah muttered.

"Okay! I'll go towards the Sorghum field and you can follow me when you think its safe to do so. I just hope I won't have to wait forever" Shungu suggested with a grin on his face. Not waiting for her reply he strode off towards the footpath leading to the field. One glance in the direction of her parents was enough to satisfy her that the coast was clear because they were so involved since the foreman and wife were the hosts. Leaving her friend stunned, Sarah pealed out of the crowd and took towards a distant footpath. Shungu could not get his eyes off her as she got closer which made her blush and nearly bumped into a stump by the path side. They strode casually through Jacaranda trees lining both sides of the footpath. The smell of the forest brought back childhood memories to Shungu. A wave of sadness overtook him as he remembered playing in the woods with his brother. Sarah not sure why he was suddenly quiet, kept her pace without disturbing Shungu's thoughts. They emerged from the trees onto a section covered with balancing rocks sloping down to the river in silence, then as if out of a spell, Shungu broke the silence:

"Sarah; I don't know how to say this, but I've had some very strange feelings from the day I first met you, strange but great feelings. I kept seeing you in my mind, missed you, wanted you . . . . I don't know . . . but I feel so good just being with you. It happened so fast that I'm still dizzy from the impact of meeting you and I think I know what it is . . . . LOVE . . . I love you Sarah!" His gaze was riveted on her face. Sarah could not speak. She wished time would stand still while she stood in this rocky area with the man she doubtlessly loved. Shungu saw the love right through her eyes and without another word, he pulled her to him and just held her tightly. When Shungu bent to kiss her she felt the whole body trembled because she had never been this close to a man and this was her first kiss (certain things you learn, but with love everything just falls in like a pattern):

"Oh Shungu, I have never felt this way for anyone before. It feels so good to be close to you . . . . I . . . love you too" She said in a husky voice. Gently he removed her arms, placed his hands on her shoulders and looked into her eyes:

"You mean that?" he asked. Yes I am sure, but . . . eeh . . . but how about Sidney?" She stammered. What about him?" Shungu asked astonished. I am afraid of him and if he finds out that you and I are seeing each other he could unleash his wrath and punish me or both of us severely. Sarah explained showing concern. Why would he do that?" He asked genuinely surprised. "Well, I'm sure you have heard about all the rumors going on in the compound about you and Sidney" she said, not looking at him.

"Sarah! What are you talking about? Could you please explain?" Shungu asked crossing his arms in front and grasping his elbows. Realizing that Shungu was completely in the dark about the rumor she decided to tell him all about it. She turned to look over the stream and hesitantly she said:

"Sidney is a homosexual" Without looking at him, she could feel his shocked reaction even though he did not speak. She went on . . . . :

"It is not your fault Shungu. You could not have known even though it is possible you could have suspected. He might not have made his advances at you yet, but believe me he will soon and if you reject his advances, you could be in a dangerous situation. People have been talking about you and him around the compound. Some even claim he spends some nights in your chalet and that you have consented to him which is why he has engaged you on prestigious jobs." Shungu exhaled loudly, the inside of his head working like a pinball machine.

"Thanks for telling me and believe me I was in the dark about all these stories. What you have just told me is beginning or rather has explained certain actions by Sidney that I could not quite figure out. Anywhere nothing has happened between us and I promise nothing will ever happen. If he as much as dares to try it with me, I'll kill him . . . I mean that" He said more to himself than to Sarah.

"But . . . but . . ." Sarah tried to say something.

"No buts. I'll kill him – Tell me how you know for sure that he is a homo?" he asked inquisitively.

"There was a man in his twenties who worked as the maintenance hand on the farm, He used to live in the cottage close to the farm house because his mother was and still is the house maid . . . ." Sarah began to explain, but Shungu interrupted:

"Wait a minute! Sidney told me that the woman that works as a maid had a son who died from cerebral malaria some years back."

"He lied. She responded without hesitation. The woman is not allowed to come to the compound or even mix with compound folks; she's virtually a prisoner even though she's a close friend with old Mrs. Stewart. Anywhere, her son became a victim of Sidney's weird emotions. The poor guy used to confide in friends and told them all the things he was made to do by Sidney and the things Sidney did to him in bed. The guy was less than a man was because he gave in to Sidney without a fight. Maybe it was because he wanted to protect his job and his mother and indeed he got gifts and favors from Sidney. The day his mother found out was the last straw for him. He could not bear it anymore. Leaving a note for his mother one night, the guy vanished only to be found two days later dangling from a tree on an electrical cord. He had committed suicide. According to my dad, there was far much more to it all. He says the night before he hanged himself, he'd confronted Sidney and declared that he no longer wanted to play his bed games, that he had a girl that he wanted to marry and was not going to let hi (Sidney) lay a hand on him again. Sidney had threatened to kill the girl and the mother if they were going to be hindrance to their affair. So rather than sacrifice the lives of his innocent family, the man killed himself instead". She finally concluded. Shungu was listening with open-mouthed awe. He felt a chill run up his spine. It was time to tread with extreme caution – nip the hovering catastrophe in the bud. Stall his moves and by any means surface and spell out his abhorrence for sodomy and all those that practice it. He kissed Sarah lightly on the lips. She moved into his arms where she felt she belonged. She lifted her face for a deeper and more exploratory kiss to seal their commitment.

"I love you so much Sarah! I have no doubt in my mind you are the one I want to settle down with – would you be ready for that?" he asked curiously. The doubts that had begun to crawl into her mind as the rumors peaked curbed. She whispered:

"Shungu, that would make me the happiest woman on this earth, but there is another problem . . ." she paused and Shungu's heart skipped a bit 'now what?' he thought.

"My father! If he is to sniff that there is something going on between you and me – he will disown me, not to mention what he will do to you – I really don't know why he hates you so much yet everyone else likes you except for the fact that they think you are Sidney's wife" she went on.

"W . . . . wh . . . . who is your father?" Shungu asked fearing for the worst.

"The farm foreman – Spinach" She answered innocently. Shungu's fists clenched and his fingernails dug into his palms 'Oh God No' he muttered to himself. Sarah looked at him. He was grim faced and when he spoke it was in clipped tones:

"H . . . . Him! Lord! Life can be so complicated" She watched him confused.

"Why? Is something wrong?" She asked. He let his eyes rove around the rocks without saying a word. The silence that followed was so sharp that it could slice a chicken's throat. Sarah moved closer to Shungu, but he moved away and started pacing around with his hands thrusted in his pockets. Sarah could see that there was something terribly wrong and she felt she was losing Shungu on each second that ticked away. She knew her father did not like Shungu but she could not understand what would make him react the way he did by the mention of her father especially when he was barely a year on the farm. Deep in her thought she did not notice that Shungu was standing right by her side and looking at her with an expression she could not place:

"Sarah . . . . My sweet little Sarah – why does life work this way . . . . My mind is spinning right now I don't know what to say or do . . . . I need time to think about all this". Shungu finally said.

"What is the matter? Please tell me, have I done something to offend you?" she begged almost in tears.

"No my dear! It is a long story and I need to think about it before I can say anything. Right now I need to go home and do some laundry". He said excusing himself. Sarah knew it was just an excuse to leave her. She did not argue, instead she held his hand and kissed his palm. Without a word she strode away with tears running down her cheeks. Shungu did not stop her, but with a heavy heart he stood watching her disappear behind the rocks. He felt so empty and very lonely. He sat on a rock and began to cry. There were so many questions he was asking with no answers. The worst one was what he was going to do about Sarah because he knew he loved her without question, but to marry her would need the parent's consent – the parents that were on his death list. He had vowed he would avenge the death of his family, now how would he do it without hurting his loved one Sarah? He thought of his abducted brother and wished he was around to help him make a decision. He sat there for uncountable hours. Finally, he decided that he would not lose Sarah because of her cruel father. He would go ahead with his plan to get rid of Stewart and Spinach without Sarah's knowledge, the sooner the better, then he would take Sarah with him and they would go to Salisbury and live happily ever after. The decision pleased him so much that he decided to immediately visit his Uncle in the compound so as to hear their views on the issue.

Sarah tried to hide her sorrow from her friend when she got back to the ground where the Gure dancer were still dancing, but Shamiso (her friend) could see that she had been crying:

"Sarah what is wrong? I am your friend and remember we promised not to have any secrets between us, but you are keeping so much from me – not to mention your boyfriend whom you never mentioned to m; did he hit you? or have you just confirmed the story about him and Sidney? Shamiso continued bugging her without giving her a chance to answer.

"Right now I am in no mood of jokes nor do I want to tell you anything so please leave me alone. I only came here because I want to get keys to the house from my mother". Sarah said in a quivering.

"What do you mean looking for your mother, she left about an hour ago, she asked me about your whereabouts and I told her I didn't know – so be prepared for trouble at home" Shamiso pointed out. Sarah's heart skipped, she definitely was in trouble. She had never been out of her mother's sight except when she was sent to the tuck-shop or at work. 'What I'm I going to say? Oh please God when am I going to rest' she thought walking towards home with Shamiso on her heels. Shamiso felt sorry for Sarah, she tried to comfort her with assuring words. Sarah started talking more to her self than to her friend:

"Shungu's reaction when I said I'm Spinach's daughter must have something to do with my father and whatever it is must be serious. If only he knew that I'm his daughter merely by name nothing more. I love Shungu and I know he loves me. I will not let my father come between Shungu and me, he will have to kill me first". Turning to Shamiso she went on:

"Do you know that people are lying about Shungu having an affair with Sidney? He is the nicest person I have ever seen and very loving. If I could denounce my father I could do it right now". She said stamping her left leg down with fury no longer caring about what lay ahead regarding her disappearance from the gathering. She didn't care what her mother would say, come hell or thunder she was ready for anything even death especially if it meant not seeing Shungu again. Shamiso did not have time to say anything because Sarah's mother was standing by the door calling out to Sarah to hurry up. They parted ways as Shamiso proceeded to her home a few huts away.

"And where have you been all this time? Whom did you expect to cook dinner Heee? The mother shouted, slapping Sarah across the face. Sarah staggered holding her face and tried to say something, but before she could, a blow hit her on the forehead and sent her to the ground. A neighbor who came and begged the mother to stop hitting her rescued her. In pain she was forced to prepare dinner and clean up which she did. As soon as she was through she took her blankets and tucked herself in without having dinner. That night Sarah was so suicidal, she thought maybe if she died she would find peace. What made her not commit suicide was the thought of Shungu; she could not imagine him with someone else. So she decided she would go and see Shungu the following day and find out if he still wanted her and if he didn't she would definitely commit suicide because there would be nothing to live for. When she finally slept, the roosters where crowing.

***

It was late when Shungu knocked at his Uncle's cardboard box door and they had long since slept. He knocked several times with no response, when he was about to walk away, a sleepy voice of his Aunt was heard. She wanted to know who was knocking at such an hour because in the compound they believed only witches moved at very odd hours. Shungu not wanting neighbors to hear or see him whispered his name through the gaps on the door and in no time the door flung open.

"Come in my son, come in – What brings you at such an hour? Has something happened?" his Aunt asked with a worried look and tone.

"Eeeh Ye . . . s, No . . . o . . ." he replied not sure what to say and went on to ask where his Uncle was.

"Your Uncle is as good as dead, when he came back from the dance he was so drunk that he could not even see the entrance to the room, he threw himself on the mat and passed out. When you started knocking I was very afraid, so I tried to wake him up but all I got was moans and groans" She said giggling. She became serious again when she noticed that Shungu was pale and seemed lost in his own world.

"Son! What is the matter? You are not yourself today, have you had problems with Sidney?" She quizzed. Shungu was sitting on a three-legged stool, looking at his fingers as though he was seeing them for the first time, after a sigh he looked up at his Aunt:

"Aunt . . . . (Pause) . . . I have decided it is now time to avenge my family, I have it all worked out, you and Uncle don't have to be involved, and I'll do it alo . . . ."

"What are you talking about son, are you out of your mind? Without our help you'll be caught before you even strike. We are old and if anything happens to us that is that, but you are still young and should keep the family name going by having children of your own". She said interrupting him.

"No! Aunt, you don't understand, this is for me, and so let me do it my way. The other thing that I wanted to say, now that you have mentioned family is that I am very much in love with a certain girl whom I want to marry but there are a few complications which I need to sort out first before I introd . . . ." Shungu explained, but was interrupted again by his Aunt:

"What girl? From where? Here in the compound? Are you crazy? Do you rea . . ."

Auntie please . . . . give me time to answer instead of just asking questions without giving me the chance to respond". Shungu cut in and went on:

"Since you insist, the girl is Sarah, Spinach's daughter". He said looking directly in her eyes for reaction. To his surprise she smiled.

"Shungu, as much as I hate to admit it, Sarah is a very nice girl with a lot of respect, she's the direct opposite of her mother and father. Almost everyone envies the poor girl, but they are afraid to talk to her because of Spinach. Believe it or not she does not like her father either. Her friend Shamiso once told me that she was saying, if she had the guts she would poison her father because of his cruelty. Anywhere I trust you know what you are doing and if ever you need help remember we are here to assist". She emphasized holding his hand. What Shungu heard from his Aunt pleased him so much that he felt like walking straight to Spinach's house and take Sarah far, far away from the miseries of the compound, but it was not to be; he had to take things one at a time. Feeling good within him, Shungu left his Aunt; he ran through the Sorghum field towards his chalet. This had been a long day and feeling so worn out, he wasted no time getting into bed and was soon asleep.

CHAPTER FIVE

THE ORPHANAGE WHERE Shungu and his brother were brought up had survived raids, vandalism and a number of boys who had been abducted by the gorilla warfare. Father James had been threatened so many times but his faith and trust in God kept him going and through everything that happened at the orphanage he came out without a scratch. Finally, his prayers had been heard and he had just received a truck donated by an American organization with bails and bails of clothes and undisclosed amount of cash to help renovate the orphanage. Missionaries took interest in the orphanage because of the hundreds of widows and children that had been orphaned by the war who had come to the orphanage to seek refuge. America and Germany played an important role in keeping the place open with their generosity in cash and kind.

Father James' usual routine on Saturdays was to conduct a church service in the morning, then in the afternoons he would go round visiting neighboring organizations to spread the word of God and seek whatever donations he could get. But on this particular day he felt quite tired after the service and so decided to sit by the porch and read his bible. The rocking cushioned bench was so comfortable that he dozed off and the bible fell from his hands. He was about to turn and make himself comfortable for an afternoon nap, when he was awakened by the echoing sound of a voice calling him. He lifted himself up looking in the direction where the sound was coming from. One of the orphans was running towards him shouting that there was someone to see him. By the time the boy had got where Father James was, he had already relayed the message. So since he had already got the message, he asked the boy who it was that wanted to see him – not that it was unusual because there were always people coming to see him with different problems or with donations. The boy did not know who it was. Father James sat back on the bench and ordered the boy to bring the stranger to the porch.

In no time, a muscular heavily built black man came in sight. Father James tried to focus who the man was, but could not figure out where he saw the man. Feeling uncertain about his intentions, Father James rose to his feet when the man was closer and extended his hand in greeting with a rather forced smile:

"I don't think we have ever met, I am Father James – what can I do for you? He asked seeing the man beam with excitement.

"Oh Father! It's me Garikayi – don't you remember? Garikayi Nhamo!" the man said tears of excitement filling his eyes. Father James immediately recognized the boy. They embraced.

"Garikayi! Shungu's brother? Ooh! My God you are great and worthy to be praised" Father James proclaimed looking up as though praying.

Garikayi was led into the house he once knew. After a refreshing bath and a good meal, Father James settled himself ready to hear Garikayi's story. This was his story – After being abducted the twelve boys, (including Garikayi) were led into the bush where they camped for over two weeks under cover waiting for a truck which was to pick them up and take them to Mozambique. During those weeks, food was not a problem but when it came to sleeping they were not allowed to use any blankets and the reason for that according to their commanders was that it was part of training and the worst was yet to come. They were told about all the evils of oppressors and urged to help fight for freedom, they all had one choice to fight or be killed and two boys that tried to run away were stubbed in cold blood as a warning to everyone who was planning on running away. The two nights they spent on the truck on the way to Mozambique were fine. Eighty miles into Mozambique, they were dropped off since the truck could not go beyond that point. The area seemed to be the meeting point because there were other abducted youths both male and female waiting for other's arrival group. Soon after their arrival, another truck arrived with over twenty youths and the march, which consisted of one hundred and five youths and twenty-one armed men, began. The long journey was tough, at night they would sleep in the tall grass with no blanket, have one meal a day. Bathing was something of the past. On numerous occasions they came in contact with wild dangerous animals. Snakes were also a menace; one of the boys was attached by an Egyptian cobra and died minutes later. Seven others fell ill during the walk and also died. There was no room for sickness, if anyone felt ill and could not go any further he or she would be left behind for the wild animals to feast upon. By the time they arrived at the Training Camp, there were sixty-three boys including Garikayi and eleven girls.

Life at the Camp was a lot better, food, blankets and water was surplus. The sleeping barracks were not too good but, compared to where they slept during the march, it was 100% better. Having been hardened by the long walk, the army training did not seem so difficult and in no time most of them where deployed in different areas of Zimbabwe to fight against the regime. Everything was tough going, lives were lost each time there were clashes between the gorillas and the soldiers. Garikayi paused as if in thought and almost as if talking to himself, said "I cannot stop wondering how I survived the close encounters with death during the years of uncountable battles, may . . . b "God . . . remember . . . God was on your side" Father James chipped in as a reminder. Garikayi continued to explain how he was later promoted to Commander and about the cease-fire that had just been declared whilst the Lancaster talks were being held in Britain and chaired by the British between the Rhodesia government led by Ian Smith, the Patriotic Front lead by Robert Mugabe and Joshua Nkomo and the special delegates appointed as mediators and to oversea that what was agreed upon was executed. So every fighter was asked to put down the weapons and cease-fire. The Commander In Chief ordered Garikayi to return to Zimbabwe from Mozambique and just be on standby to await the outcome of the talks. The talks were a success and there was a possibility of free and fair elections in the near future. Having been given two weeks off that is when he decided to come and see Father James in hope of seeing Shungu.

Father James who had been listening quietly, breathed a sigh and took Garikayi's hands in his and asked Garikayi to close his eyes for a prayer – a prayer of thanks to the mighty God because to survive such endeavors would only be by the grace of God. After the prayer, Father James took Garikayi on a tour of the Orphanage, showing him the improvements and explaining about Shungu's whereabouts. When he mentioned The Hamilton Farm Garikayi stopped in his tracks unsure he heard right:

"Father! Did you say The Hamilton Farm?" He asked puzzled.

"Yeah! The Hamilton Farm, Do you know the Farm?" He asked also puzzled. Garikayi immediately remembered that Father James did not know the true story of how they came to be with the German Couple, so he shook his head in denial, and then went on to ask:

"Father, Are you sure he's fine? Whilst at war, we had quite a number of youths who voluntarily came to join the gorilla welfare saying it was better to die fighting than to be gunned down like a dog on the farm, a . . . nd . . . . th . . . is particular farm, I'm sure . . . was one of them" Garikayi said exaggerating hoping to get more information out of Father James.

"Well, I heard so many stories myself, but I understand it is not as bad anymore, since the son Sidney took over from his father Stewart. Sidney also told me that he likes Shungu very much and they seem to get along very well – he is actually an assistant to Sidney" Father explained.

"You mean he is the foreman?" Garikayi asked wanting to get the facts straight.

"Oh no! Spinach is the foreman, but Shungu is only answerable to Sidney, which to my understanding, has made Spinach worried about his position being given to Shungu since Sidney does not seem to like him" he replied with emphasis. Garikayi knowing the situation at the farm, still had doubts about the safety of his brother. He so much wanted to ask about Stewart, but thought against it because he knew that would raise suspicion on how he came to know Stewart. Instead, he asked if it was possible to see Shungu before he left.

"Oh yes, that is not a problem, I can drive you there myself" Father James suggested, nodding.

"No . . . no! That won't be necessary" Garikayi refused quickly afraid there would be too many questions asked.

"Son! What's eating you? You seem to be acting strangely since I mentioned the farm; could there be something you are hiding from me? Right now you say you don't want me to take you to your brother, how will you find the place without my help? Besides, if I go with you there are chances he could be given sometime off to be with you – don't you see?" he asked suspiciously. Garikayi felt bad about lying to Father James because he got both of them where they were at that time, without him agreeing to take them in when the German Couple was leaving, they could probably have been dead. He was so confused and did not know how Father James would react to the truth, he also thought, if he did not tell him the truth it would be so difficult for him to see Shungu away from the farm. Garikayi was relieved when Father James was called for a phone call. That gave him time to think about the situation. Finally he thought against telling him the truth in case it changed the stance between them. When Father James came back, Garikayi was ready with answers.

"Sorry Son I had to take care of business, So! Where were we?" he asked sitting down and making himself comfortable.

"You had asked me why I did not want to go with you to the farm" Garikayi reminded him and went on:

"You see Sir, Whilst in the war, we had a lot of conflicts with farmers, and they were not at all friendly, so I just presumed that if I went there with you things would be bad for my brother especially with the fact that I am one of the freedom fighters, so I think the best way is for me to write him a letter which I would just give you to give him when next you visit the farm. I will put my address for him to write me back. In the mean time, I will go back and will be back in about two weeks" Garikayi explained convincingly. Father James was still not convinced, but he let it pass and agreed to take the letter to Shungu over the weekend which was four days away. Garikayi spent the night at the Orphanage and left very early in the morning for Salisbury.

Father James being an honest man, who kept his promises, left for the farm on Sunday afternoon with Shungu's letter. The drive was tiring, especially for him, being eighty-four years old. When he got to the Farm, it was deserted. He went to the farmhouse and found the house maid busy ironing clothes. He inquired about the whereabouts of the Stewart's and was told of their absence until Wednesday. He proceeded to Shungu's cabin and found it deserted too. Not wanting to waste time, he took the letter, shoved it under the door and was on his way back to town.

CHAPTER SIX

S HUNGU WAS THE kind of person that always opted to be early or too early for work and since he started working on the farm, not once had he started late. But like they say – never say never, on this day he was in the middle of a good dream when he was suppose to be up and so he overslept and had it not been for the maid who came looking for him with a message from Sidney, it could have been disaster especially with Spinach making it his business to see that work is done during his boss's absence. The sound of a knock at first, seemed to be part of his dream, but when it became persistent that's when he realized that there was someone at the door. He lazily opened one eye then the other, and then reluctantly stretched for his old wristwatch, which Father James had given him. One look at the watch made him jump out of bed like a buck suddenly aware a Lion was creeping towards it. He grabbed his trousers and in haste wore it the other way round, took a shirt and darted towards the door whilst putting the shirt on. He opened the door in time to see the maid walking away. Shungu had to call out to her, to come back. The maid gave him the message and when he was about to close the door, the maid noticed the letter on the floor and pointed it to Shungu. Having no time, he picked it up, tried to thrush it in his trousers and found the pockets where the other way. He rushed in to turn the trousers and without wasting time dashed out toward the Tool Shed.

Spinach was leaning by the Shed, watching Shungu hurrying down the path. His face had a 'this will be news to the master's ears' expression. Shungu brushed passed him without a word and immediately got down to business. Spinach, swore under his breath and spat to the ground before storming away, leaving a streak of dust behind. Shungu waited until Spinach was out of sight and quickly pulled out the letter, which he thought, was from Sarah. He ripped the envelope open and the name he saw at the bottom of the letter made him freeze with shock. Hands shaking and feeling weak to stand, he sat down. He slowly began to read the letter from his brother Garikayi. The news in the letter brought so much joy to Shungu, he leaped, tangoed and looked up as though in prayer . . . . :

"Good Lord! Good Lord! Thank you for taking care of my brother . . . . I am not alone after-all! God you are great . . . Oh my" Shungu went on with praise. He so much wanted to share this news with someone, but unfortunately everyone was busy working and he had a lot of catching up to do since he started late. That day if Shungu did any work, it was not properly done. 'Sarah, if only I could share my excitement with you and maybe if I accomplish my mission this week, we could go back to Salisbury with my brother when he comes, get married, have children' These were thoughts running in Shungu's mind.

Shungu looked at his watch and it was 4:55 PM. He immediately started packing the tools away, ready to call it a day . . . .

"And where do you think you are going so soon? Have you forgotten that you started late and so you must knock off late?" Came Spinach's voice from behind. Shungu paused for a while, and then turned round to face Spinach:

"Now you listen old fool! The time I start and finish is none of your damn business, and if you think you can push me around like you did with my fa . . . . with the people in the compound, FORGET. Do yourself a favor and report me as soon as the boss comes. One more thing, next time you try to cross my path, I'll make sure you cross it for the last time – DO YOU HEAR ME!" Shungu shouted holding Spinach's shirt by the collar. This act came as a shock to Spinach who was used to having his way and had never been threatened by any farm worker. His eyes nearly popped out with fright. When Shungu pushed him away, he staggered and fell, without a word he rose and disappeared the way he had come. Shungu had wanted to get rid of Spinach right there, since there was no one in sight except the two of them but he quickly decided against it because that was his work place and that would certainly make him the first suspect. Locking the tool shed he headed home deep in thoughts.

After a bath and dinner, Shungu settled himself down to write a letter to his brother, which he meant to give to the tuck shop delivery driver to go and post for him in town. Before he could write a paragraph, there was a knock on the door. Thinking it could be no other than Sidney, he quickly hid the letter before heading for the door. Seeing Sarah standing there made his tongue hang out with disbelief. For a while, time stood still. Shungu was so stunned that he could not speak; he just stood there unable to believe who was before him. Sarah not sure whether she was welcome or not, stood by the doorstep waiting to be invited in. As though coming out of a comma, Shungu stood aside and using his hand gave Sarah a sign to come in and slowly closed the door:

"Sarah! Is it really you? Do you know how much I have missed you? Oh Sarah!" he said taking her into his arms. Tears of joy filled Sarah's eyes; she had thought Shungu was no longer interested in her. Feeling Shungu's warmth and his muscular arms around her made Sarah feel so secure and felt life was worth living after all, suicidal thoughts erased immediately . . .

"My darling Shungu, words cannot express how much I have missed you nor how empty I felt thinking you no longer wanted me, it wa . . . ." Shungu interrupted her with a kiss that left them both breathless. He led her into the combined living/bed room and they sat on the edge of the bed:

"Sarah tell me something; won't your parents be wondering where you are right now?" Shungu asked afraid of the worst for Sarah's sake.

"Oh no they won't. I prepared super for them and my father left for the beer-hall and my mother had gone to bed, so I sneaked out without being noticed, I had to come and find out what was happening since we parted on a sad note yesterday". She said looking directly in his eyes.

"My love for you has actually tripled since yesterday. Having you in my arms was, is and will always be my dream. I want you to be by my side always" Shungu assured her, meaning every word. He went on:

I am planning on leaving the farm and go to Salisbury where my brother lives and I was hoping you would come with me si . . . ." Not waiting for him to finish his statement, Sarah got up, hugged and kissed him with excitement . . . . :

"Mudiwa wangu (my darling) that will make me the happiest woman in the world. I know my parents would not approve, but that does not bother me, I would just leave without telling them because as you know my father is cruel and he treats me like any other servants here on the farm. I was actually planning on running away to anywhere than to spend the rest of my life with that evil man. You have no idea how cruel he is because you are quite new here – believe it or not he has had families murdered by boss Stewart with his lies" She explained emotionally. There was no doubt in Shungu's mind about Sarah's love for him and he felt she was the woman for him. He found it so hard to believe that such an evil man can bare such a soft, kind and loving woman like Sarah. He was tempted to tell her the truth about his family, but decided it was not the time yet.

The two lovers engaged in passionate romance, treading steadily and careful not to indulge in the actual sex for fear of a pregnancy that both were not ready for. They were so busy with each other that they did not hear a tap on the door. After two knocks, Sidney stumbled into the dimly lit chalet. Before him was the fondling couple who only learned of his presence when the parcel he was holding fell from his hands to the concrete floor with a loud clattering sound. Shungu had no reason to quickly disengage from the intimate moment, but did so all the same. What followed was what he'd later recall as a volcanic eruption. Sidney, with quick deft movements sprung upon Sarah, yanked her on her feet, and slapped her viciously across the face, then shoved her violently against the wall. Shungu's blood raced, he dived at Sidney's throat and began to squeeze with demonic strength. Sidney let go of Sarah and with his entire mighty, drove his elbow into Shungu's guts. His grip around Sidney's neck loosened as he reeled backwards and folded on his knees desperately sucking in air that had been displaced by the thump. While in that position, Sidney advanced towards him aiming to splitter his scull with the iron bar he'd grabbed from the closet rails. Sarah's scream somehow lifted the blinding cloud of rage that had engulfed him and slowly brought him back to his senses. Standing over Shungu with one arm raised, he let the hand drop to his side, still holding the iron bar. Shungu slowly rose to his feet and with hate in his eyes, looked at Sidney:

"Why did you do that?" he asked hoarsely. Sidney who had turned to face the door where Sarah was, spun round with lightning speed. When he spoke, his voice was seasoned with maddening fury . . . :

"Who are you to question what I do? And, who told you to bring slats into this chalet hah? This chalet belongs to the farm! It belongs to me with all that is in it and that includes you!" he roared, digging his thumb into his chest.

"She's not a whore sir, and if I may remind you sir, I work for you but I do not belong to you, I . . . ." He replied taking a quick glance at Sarah who sat hunched her face in her palms sobbing. Sidney cut his statement short:

"Shut up! No native talks to me like that – Do you hear – No one. You open that beak of yours again and I will turn it to ground beef" Sidney hissed right in Shungu's face. He looked dangerous and his face had gone a bright red with fury, this Shungu noted with a chill because Sidney's eyes were glittering in the dim light. He turned to Sarah who was trying by all means to hide her face to avoid recognition.

"What is your name and whose daughter are you?" Sidney asked bending over Sarah with both his hands on his waistline. Sarah fearing for his family, did not respond, she just kept facing down with her arms blocking any other slaps to the face. Sidney not wanting to waste time on Sarah grabbed her by the hand and pushed her towards the door. Sarah, terrified, scrambled out of the chalet. Shungu tried to go after her but Sidney stuck his frame on the doorway and pushed him back onto the bed. Boiling inside with anger, he complied because he thought Sidney was capable of anything and so the best was to watch his strides . . .

"You'd better get this straight. I did not give you this chalet to use as a harlot territory and that girl better pray I don't see her tomorrow because that will be her last day on earth. You belong to me and only me" He stressed before going on in a much softer tone that surprised Shungu . . . . :

"Besides . . . I don't see what you find attractive in a woman. Women are a menace, a pain in the ass, they cause nothing but trouble. If you let me, I can teach you things that you will no doubt find to be much, much more intriguing and you will discover true ecstasy. Wholesome bliss, not in women but in . . . . in . . . . damn! Why do to want to lose great opportunities. To sacrifice all the security, a bright future with more money for a mare compound trash? Think of all the things that you could benefit from me if you stuck with me . . . . don't you see?" Shungu had been listening to all this absent-mindedly. His only desire was to get rid of Sidney quickly and bolt after Sarah before she got home. He wanted to comfort her, kiss her, love her and most of all protect her. He looked up at Sidney who was looking down at him with a glint of deep desire . . . .

"Shungu . . . . Oh . . . . Shungu you are beautiful . . . . I love you" He whispered bending down toward Shungu. Shungu rolled to the other side of the bed and got to his feet is a split second . . . .

"If you'll excuse me, I want to pack my things. I am leaving at daybreak. I did not realize that when I bargained with you, I had also bargained my entire self" Shungu said firmly. Sidney stood still and did not speak for a while, his eyes still fixed at Shungu as if ticking to explode but instead, released a mirthless laugh and then spoke . . . :

"And where will you go! Back to the Clergyman?" he mocked.

"I might try Salisbury; see if I can get a job there. Even if I have to sleep on the side walk, I'll be fine because I will not be owned by anyone" Shungu replied confidently.

"You must love that whore very much . . . . If I gave you $1000.00 would you promise to stay and work for me and promise never to talk to that girl again? Sidney asked in an almost begging tone.

"Sir, you don't seem to have heard what I said. I love my job and job only, but when you talk of working for you, you mean I work in the workshop during the day and you work on me during the night, and that will not happen, besides, Sir, freedom is priceless. I could be a millionaire but without freedom I won't be worth a penny" he explained, trying to make his boss see sense.

"What freedom are you talking about? Are you going political on me now?" Sidney asked.

"No . . . No Sir, I mean freedom to at-least enjoy some privacy, befriend whoever I want" Shungu said wearily.

"You're a fool! Stupid son of a bitch! Get out of my chalet right now and be on your way this very minute before I scatter your useless brain" Sidney threatened, suddenly transformed into a deadly viper once more. Shungu's heart skipped a bit, he knew he had to do something fast or else he was doomed . . . :

"Sir, please don't throw me out. Give me at-least time to think about the whole thing. Your request came as a shock to me because being my boss nothing of this sort ever occurred to me and its something I have never done, so don't you see that what I need is time to adjust, besides I like you and you know it" Shungu begged, trying to gain time to accomplish his own mission. The last line "I like you" is all that

Sidney heard and without hesitation, gave Shungu until the following evening to think about it. Before he left, he caressed Shungu's chest and kissed him good night. Seeing him walk out and close the door behind him was such a relief for Shungu. He peeped to see if his boss was gone and saw the last glimpse of his shadow disappearing into the night towards his house. He sat back on the bed numb with panic. He realized he had been entangled in a similar situation to the one that saw the housemaid's son kill himself. The only difference was that the poor man had been sodomized on countless occasions before he decided to protest, where he could have made life easier for himself and his family by simply continuing to please Sidney. Unlike Shungu's case where Sidney was still campaigning to win access and persuade him to play along but even then, the life of an innocent girl was in grave danger and so was his own if he did not comply. Shungu knew he was not the product that saw suicide as the easiest solution, his only way out was to come up with a plan, which at that moment was not a priority. First he needed to see if Sarah was okay, which meant going to the Compound at that very hour. He grabbed a sweater and before opening the door, took another peep through the window to see if the coast was clear then quickly dashed out.

Unknown to him, Sarah, a quick thinking, and intelligent girl had known where the incident of an hour ago was going to lead. After she left the chalet, she ran off in the direction of the compound weeping hysterically. Half way there, she had branched off to a near-by baobab tree. Gradually she had ceased crying and began to think. Crying was not going to get her anywhere she'd thought. She wondered what had happened back at the chalet after she'd been ordered out. Even though she feared for Shungu, she new he was a real man. None of all the heavily muscled men she knew around the farm had ever dared to stand up to Sidney even if he booted their wives for whatever reasons, but, Shungu had gone for the white man's throat. Unfortunately Sidney was physically stronger than Shungu; otherwise he'd most definitely been choked to death. This she had seen in his eyes as he piled pressure on the man's thick neck. Sarah also knew from Sidney's past that he usually spared the men he adored preparing to eliminate those that stood in the way of his advances and in this case – herself. But with Shungu's obstinacy, she feared he could be driven into thoughtlessness and act on impulse. So, she decided to sneak back and hid in the bushes to see what was happening. After what seemed to be a lifetime, she saw the white man walk out and trot towards his house. Afraid that he could be coming back and also fearing for the worst in the chalet, she remained hidden, not sure what to do next. It was at this time that Shungu opened the door. He looked left and right before walking out and with a quick step headed for the compound. He did not notice Sarah who was now standing and leaning against a tree.

"Shungu! I'm here!" Sarah called out. He stopped short in his tracks and quickly rushed to where Sarah was. He released a sigh of relief and went straight into her open arms. Neither said a word. They held each other so tight that her breasts crushed on his chest. She was cautious when he unzipped her dress, but resistance had gone out of her and was replaced by desire she could not explain. She moaned softly when he caressed her firm nipples with his tongue. Shungu's manhood was on the verge of exploding with desire. He pulled Sarah's hand slowly and brought it down to his manhood and as soon as she touched his private parts, hell broke loose . . . . next thing they were sprawled on the grass, the fear of pregnancy forgotten, feeling the whole world was theirs and no one else mattered. They locked into intimacy that brought pleasure that neither of them had ever experienced. The pain of virginity did not hinder her from enjoying neither ecstasy nor the fulfillment of womanhood.

Sarah began to feel uneasy about Shungu's silence after their love making because he rolled back and lay there facing the sky without a word for almost ten minutes, which to Sarah was almost a lifetime. She wondered whether she did not please him sexually or whether he was beginning to have second thoughts about her since she had given him what he wanted. Whilst deep in those thoughts, Shungu pulled her to him and wrapped his hands around her . . . :

"Sarah . . . I love you with all my heart, you've made me feel like a man and I know that without you, my life would be empty. I don't want Sidney to place his claws on you my darling ever again because I know if he did I would kill him" he assured her, as though knowing what she was thinking.

"Oh Shungu! I love you more than anything in this world; you have made me the happiest woman with your words. You are my one and only 'ntil death parts us" She also assured him.

During the course of their conversation, Shungu decided to confide in Sarah, he told her everything that happened to his family through to the time he came to the farm, but, did not mention his reason for accepting the job at the farm – VEGEANCE. He also told her about his Uncle and Auntie that were on the farm whom Sarah knew very well. The story made Sarah so emotional and all she could do was cry. When Shungu finished the story, his mind was racing, everything was back in his mind and that very minute he decided that it was time to fulfill his father's wish. Sarah, who had been crying silently, pulled Shungu's hand and whispered:

"I know there's nothing I can do to change what happened, but I want you to know that what ever you decide to do, I will be on your side. My father has had so many families killed and believe it or not, if it was not for my mother, I'm sure he could have killed me too because he has no care for me whatsoever. I hate him just as much and so many times I have wished him dead. If fathers could be auctioned, I could have auctioned mine a long time ago. (After a pause) Shu . . . ngu . . . . W . . . hy . . . don't we just elope this very moment and go as far as we possibly can. There's too much pain around this farm. May . . . ."

"Sarah; running away will not solve the problem, the only way is to stop Stewart, Sidney and your father's cruelty once and for all. Trust me things are going to be fine sooner than you think. If I survived the massacre of my family, I will survive this one. Since Sidney is not going to do anything until tomorrow evening as per his last words and knowing that his times of coming to the chalet are well after 9 PM, we should meet here around 7 PM, by then I will have knitted out a plan". Shungu said, interrupting Sarah.

"I understand what you are saying, but remember I have to work tomorrow and Sidney usually comes to check on the chickens. Suppose he recognizes me what will I do? My father will kill me if he hears about this. You know how much he hates you. I am so scared". Shungu knew that she was right, he had not thought about that. After a while he came up with a plan, which he prayed and hoped, would work. He escorted Sarah to his Uncle's place and asked them to take care of her and keep her out of sight until he came back. He gave them money to help with food. His uncle knew that he was putting himself in danger, but for Shungu, he was willing to do anything because he trusted and loved the boy very much and Sarah was one girl they liked and always wondered how a beast could produce such a lamb. Sarah on the other hand liked the old couple, who were already making her feel at home – a peaceful home she had never known.

Shungu trotted back to his empty cold chalet. His mind was reeling with plans of getting even with the Stewart family, Spinach and leaving the farm. 'When Sidney comes tomorrow I am going to be ready for him, I'll make sure he does not walk out of here alive – it's either him or me. No man will touch my body; this body is for Sarah alone. Once he's out of the way the rest will be easy' He thought. Knowing that Sarah was safe made him feel comfortable and with Sarah on his mind, he fell asleep.

CHAPTER SEVEN

THE STEWART FAMILY had cut their holiday short because of the disturbing commotion that were taking place in most parts of the Country since the announcement two days ago that the War was over, and General Elections were scheduled to take place within a year. Salisbury being the capital city had much more excitement, which most whites took as disturbances, and the fact that there were more blacks in areas that were just for whites and seeing blacks drinking clear beer without fear of being seen was cause for alarm form most whites. So not wanting to spend a day longer in Salisbury, they drove back to their Kingdom – The Seven Stud Farm.

As soon as Sidney got back to the farm, he thought of giving Shungu what he thought would be a pleasant surprise, but, turned out to be a disappointment. After walking out of the chalet, he went and stood by his truck, lit a cigarette. The picture of Shungu's muscular body vivid in his mind, he vowed nobody would stand in his way:

'I will not let that bony good for nothing compound trash blind my boy from reality, I know he loves me too, but could not admit it. I bet he's looking forward to tomorrow evening as much as I am. But, I am not going to take any chances with that stupid girl. So first thing tomorrow morning, I am going to ask Spinach to call for a meeting and will want everyone on the farm to attend without fail, and during that meeting I will get the girl and deal with her accordingly' he thought. These thoughts pleased him enough to blot out the coming Independence for all races and colors.

Stewart aware of what lay ahead, sat in the living room waiting for his son who knowing his habits, knew he had gone to the chalet. He had tried to discourage him but to no avail, and old as he was, all fighting had gone out of him, so he simply watched and was glad, that the running of the farm was not affected by his actions. When Sidney walked in, he was surprised to see his father in the living room, which was unusual, since he fell ill well over a year ago.

"Dad, what's up?" he asked puzzled

"Sidney, I'll get straight to the point. Do you know what Independence for a black person means? I'll tell you – It means they'll start demanding for better wages, better standard of living, equal rights etc and if their demands are not met, they will strike and not work. What I'm trying to tell you is, you better start using your brain instead of fooling around with that ape in the chalet. You know I depend on you to run this farm, as you know, your brother is not interested in the farm business and I on the other hand, am not well, not to mention being old. If you . . . ."

"Father, do not worry about all that, nothing of that sort is going to happen here. If it means firing everyone and employing new laborers, I'll do just that. Spinach knows how to deal with the hot heads and besides, I have already planned to have a meeting with all the laborers tomorrow morning, you may come too if you wish." Sidney said interrupting his father and giving him a pat on the shoulder to assure him that he knew what he was doing. Stewart, not wanting to say anything more, got to his feet with his walking stick and slowly walked to his bedroom. Sidney took three shots of whisky before turning in for the night.

Spinach that had gone to bed without eating because he had come home too drunk to even sit up was busy harassing his wife to warm up his cold food when Sidney banged on the door. Not expecting his boss at such an early hour he shouted . . . :

"Hey! Get away from my door before I squash you like a cockroach, is that a wa . . . ."

"You come out here before you become the cockroach" Sidney shouted back, cutting spinach's sentence short and pushing the door open. The minute he saw his boss, the hangover drained out of him and he became as sober as a priest . . . :

"Yes Bass . . . Yes I am coming" he said putting his shoes on and dashing out.

"I want you to tell everyone to go to the Open Grounds for a meeting. I will be there in thirty minutes. I mean everybody, if I see anyone in the compound in thirty minutes you will be in trouble" Sidney ordered. No sooner had he left, Spinach spread the word like fire and in no time, the grounds were packed by everyone except Sarah who was left hidden in the hut. Spinach saw Shungu who was about to start the Tractor and shouted at him to switch the machine off and go to the grounds immediately, but Shungu not wanting to take orders from Spinach ignored him, which made Spinach angry.

"Idiot! Who do you think you are around here? Bass Sidney wants everyone including you to be at the grounds in ten minutes. Believe me boy, your days are numbered around here.". Spinach said giving Shungu an evil eye. When Shungu realized that Spinach was saying the truth, his heart skipped – he switched off the engine and with so many questions going through his mind, he walked towards the grounds. 'What could be the matter, has Sidney changed his mind about tonight? Is he trying to find Sarah or has Spinach reported her missing?' he thought. Having no answers and with an uneasy feeling he stood next to his Aunt and Uncle who told him that Sarah was safe and sound. He asked them if they knew what the meeting was all about but neither of them knew.

In all the years of the Seven Stud Farm, no meeting was ever held with the peasants, except orders that came from Spinach. Every peasant, including Spinach, was wondering what the meeting was all about. The noise was deafening, with each and everyone giving their own opinion of what was to come. Some thought the Stud had been sold and their boss was about to ask them to leave, some thought Spinach was at it again and the ever hopeful thought there were being advised about an increment in their wages etc. Almost everyone became tense when they saw Sidney's truck a distance away. Spinach, as usual, wanting praise from his boss, started ordering everyone to sit down and be quiet. This was not necessary because silence had already prevailed with tension. The tension grew even more when they saw Stewart whom they had last seen nearly two years ago, when he had come to discipline (as he called it) one of the peasants whom Spinach had reported as being lazy. The man was beaten until he could not stand on his feet. He was bed-ridden for three months then later died from luck of medication.

Sidney got out of the truck and taking his own time, lit a cigarette before facing the tired, worn-out faces that sat before him. Stewart sat in the truck, with the door open and his legs hanging out.
"I have been doing a lot of thinking lately and I have decided to change a few things around here. Firstly, I no longer require the services of old laborers because my mission is to boost business not to take care of a bunch of aged, weak bones (he paused and looked at Spinach who was sitting close-by). Secondly, from now on, I am going to follow my father's way of running the farm – with an iron fist because I can see, you are all beginning to relax and forgetting your boundaries. Thirdly, I want the girl that I saw sneaking around at the Chalet to come forward before I assign Spinach to look for her, because, if I do, she'll have no legs to stand on". The third statement made those with daughters panic and most eyes were looking at the girls wanting to see which girl it was, but no one went forward.
"Now listen you good for nothing baboons! I hate to be made a fool and I am warning you that if I come to you, you will wish you were never born" Sidney shouted getting angry (a pause) then went on . . .

"Okay! I want every parent with a daughter to stand up with your daughter or daughters; remember my father here knows each and everyone's children". At that moment, it downed on Spinach that he had not seen his daughter at all that morning. He looked at his wife who was frantically looking around for her daughter but to no avail. Spinach began to sweat and when he tried to stand up, his legs gave in and he fell. No one thought much of it; they just thought it was old age taking its toll. Shungu was frantic with worry and was trying to think of how to save the innocent people. He knew that the next question was going to be finding out where Spinach's daughter was, which meant they could search every hut until they found her and he knew what the Stewarts where capable of doing.

Sidney looked at all the girls that were standing but did not see the one he was looking for.

"Spinach! Are those the only girls in the compound?" he asked pointing.

"No . . . no bass . . . . There is also . . . my daughter, I don't know where she is" Spinach stammered in a quivering voice.

"Oh! So it is your daughter haa! I am going to . . . ." Sidney said pocking Spinach on his forehead. His statement was interrupted by the sound of a vehicle. Sidney hopped on to the back of his truck to see whose car was approaching. He noticed that the car was a Grey Land-rover.

The approaching vehicle held everyone's attention as it came down the rise negotiating boulders and maneuvering towards the mortally crew. As soon as the vehicle came to a halt alongside Sidney's truck, the driver climbed out and four others who were in the back jumped out. All five black men were in khaki apparel and looked mean projecting their presence with maximum effect. Sidney's riveted crowd watched closely as the driver made towards them – hands thrust deep in his pockets. There was something about the guy that bore right though Sidney, his eyes, an aura of weirdness and danger that he couldn't help but sense. The man approached Sidney with an extended hand . . .

"My name is Hokoyo (watch out), I am sorry if we interrupted anything,

"I'm glad we find you all here – the basses (meaning bosses) and their subjects all in one grouping" he said smiling a weary grin.

"Who the hell are you and what do you want here? Do you realize you are intruding on private property?" Sidney screamed angrily.

"As I said – the name is Hokoyo. You can bet your last dollar I bring you hell, your nightmare has just begun" Hokoyo continued his face taking on a dark menacing look. Stewart who had been talking to his wife on the radio transmitter thundered onto the scene hand reaching for his holstered .38 police special.

"What's going on here?" He roared. Hokoyo slowly spun round to face the white farmer completely unmoved by the pistol in his hand.

"Put that little piece of iron away – you good for nothing piece of garbage" Hokoyo growled.

"Don't do anything silly Dad – those men in the truck have got all their Kalashnikov's pointing at you" Sidney said helplessly. Stewart swung a confused eye at the truck and as the realization of the hopelessness of his position dawned on him, he thawed but not before trying a feeble tack at nerve.

"You guys are using a Rhodesian Infantry Battalion truck, whose command are you under? All I need to do is radio Lieutenant Jenkins and you will all be on shooting squad" There was a roar of laughter from all five men and for a moment the ugly face of Hokoyo looked somehow less frightening. He laughed the loudest with his mouth wide open in a mockery fashion without care about showing his yellow scattered teeth that needed serious dental attention.

"Now that is what I call a joke – you are still sleeping 'ant you; Jenikins (Jenkins) is now history just as Rhodesia is now history, he will be lucky to even get the chance to pack his belongs before our other comrades take over and as you can see we are already in possession of the vehicles" Hokoyo pointed out still laughing and poking Stewart's forehead. Then he derided pacing with firm confidence the clearing. He looked the crowd over. The faces that met his glare spoke of confusion, anticipation and shock – shock at seeing a black man sassing down the almighty Stewart.

Amongst the dumbfounded crowd was Shungu whose gaze was fixed beyond Hokoyo's shoulders at the imposing figure of a man who had just stepped out of the truck. Shungu was the only one who was not put off by the change of bloodshed or by the dangers of flirting with these potential killers, the whole scenario excited him. 'Something was vaguely familiar about the man standing by the truck' he thought. His pre-occupation was disturbed as Hokoyo's words snapped him back to the moment.

"The war is over" Hokoyo was saying, and the farm laborers were now taking a keen interest in the ugly African who had instilled so much fear in their boss. The man was a gorilla welfare leader armed to the teeth and ready for anything. Hokoyo went on addressing Stewart and Sidney:

". . . And I am proud to announce to you that our people are now free people. News of this is all over the print and electronic media, beats me how you could have missed it but am not surprised because you'll obviously be too absorbed riding hard on your slaves to watch TV". Without turning, Hokoyo pointed a long finger at the truck and went on sarcastically:

"That truck was indeed a Rhodesia Infantry Truck but not anymore. We the comrades are now in charge and this is now Zimbabwe not Rhodesia" He pulled out a 9mm mouser automatic from a shoulder holster and fired two shots in the air sending Sidney scurrying for cover which he failed to find and slumped to the ground from fear. Hokoyo smiled with a very unattractive smile.

"That was to introduce to you my Commander." He turned to the man leaning against the truck –

"Comrade, it's your floor" Hokoyo said with a salute.

The man stepped forward, He was immensely strong, and his body bore the scars of war. He paused by Stewart and Sidney, his eyes icy cold and without warning shoved them both so hard that Stewart sprawled to the ground but Sidney just staggered.

"The times of cheap labor are gone, so you better sit down quietly until asked to speak or else you will find yourselves knocking on devil's door sooner that you think". The words were like a knife thrusting in Stewart's already poor heart – he stiffened and slowly pulled his son down who was just as afraid and shifting his feet nervously. Since none of the laborers had been to school except Shungu no one heard what Hokoyo or the other stranger said. When they saw Stewart and his son sitting down they followed suit their faces showing bewilderment. Not wanting to keep them in suspense much longer, the man introduced himself as Tichakunda (we shall conquer) Commander of the Armed Forces, Hokoyo, as the Commander's Assistant, Mheni (lightning) the Labor Officer and the other two as bodyguards namely Hondo (war), Shumba (lion). After a pause Tichakunda drew a long breath and cleared his throat fixing a hostile glance at Stewart making Stewart shiver. He took two steps towards Stewart then as if out of a stance restrained himself and grimaced . . . He began to speak in Shona the native language . . . which the farm owners had no problem understanding –

"We have brought you good news. Fear the white man no more, we fought the war of oppression and we have won, it is time to celebrate the end of the Liberation Struggle" The shouts of joy that came from the workers were deafening. On impulse nearly everyone got to their feet, somewhere jumping up and down, somewhere dancing, somewhere throwing their ragged shirts in the air and some where hugging each other. Elderly people cried with joy, this good news could not have come at a better moment when something sinister was about to happen – another massacre of some family. Shungu was so excited that without thought, ran to the compound to get Sarah. In no time, he was running back, with Sarah on his heels. Spinach, on the other hand, had mixed feeling because he knew that the workers hated him and he knew that the first thing they would want to do is kill him. He did not stand up like the rest of them; instead he sat with his hands behind his head. Sidney had an idea this was coming but did not expect it to come this way. He had heard the rumors when he went to Salisbury with his family. His face was ashen and beads of sweat where beginning to form on his forehead. Stewart sat rigid his eyes bloodshot red and full of hate.

"Order Please, Order!" Hokoyo shouted giving a sign for everyone to sit down. As soon as silence was restored Tichakunda went on . . . .

"First and fore-most, I do not go around the farms passing the good word that you've just heard, reason being that I have my subordinates who are doing that, but, this farm is exceptional that is why I decided to come personally. Why I say this farm is exceptional is because this farm holds terrible memories of my childhood" (he paused) seeing the bewildered look on everyone's face including the men he had come with. He continued . . .

"Not only does it hold bad memories, it also happens to be the farm of my birth. My real name is Kuda and I am informed my kid brother Rutendo is on this farm but now goes with the name Shungu" He paused yet again seeing the shocked expressions on everyone's face. Shungu's mind was racing, his heart thumping hard blows against his chest. 'It can't be' he whispered to himself – loud enough for those close to him to hear. All eyes were focused on Shungu including those of Sidney and his father. A silent prayer escaped the white man's lips as he tried to figure out which family were the two boys from because he had murdered quite a number of families, the many incidences played back in his mind. He did not even see Shungu dart past him to throw himself in his brother's open arms. It was an emotional moment. The farm workers began to buzz and whisper in undertones. After a very lengthy embrace and sobs from Shungu, Kuda pulled free and still holding his kid brother's shoulder he turned to Spinach:

"Now! Spinach! Yes you Spinach" he yelled at the jelly legged foreman.

"Come forth and stand at the center here! That goes for you Stewart and your Son – Come On! Move we don't have all day!" The three-some assembled.

"Spinach! Stewart! Do you remember us? That's right we are Nhamo's boys. The boys who survived when you; Spinach and your Boss slaughtered our family. My mom, my pap and my sisters – that you butchered without mercy – Now is payback time" Garikayi hissed spiting in Stewart's face. Stewart whose weak heart could not take any more shock was pounding uncontrollably. He remembered who Nhamo was and how he had wiped out the family as he thought he had done not knowing there were other children who I'm sure if he had known could have tracked down and gunned too. This was too much for his heart and it gave in – he collapsed. Sidney knelt down – a worried look on his face, he felt the old man's pulse and was relieved to discover the old man was still breathing.

"My father need attention, I've got to get his pills" Sidney said pleadingly.

"Let him be!" Hokoyo bellowed. "Your father massacred the Commander's family and enjoyed every minute of it – why should we care. Best he dies because If he lives we plan on putting him through a painful run down and kill him slowly, so slow that he will beg us to finish him. So thank your stars if he passes on from a mere heart flop"

"Our parents were left by the road side to be a feast for vultures and game – let the dog die!" Kuda added biting his lower lip. Turning to the crowd he yelled:

"What shall we do to these murderous swine's?"

"Kill them! Kill them! Burn them alive! Spinach must die!" came the loud shouts and chants, others picking sticks and rocks or anything they could lay their hands on. A terrified Spinach dismantled on to the ground and messed his pants.

"Please Mister, do not kill us. So many times I got a beating from my husband Spinach for trying to talk him out of his evil ways including the day he reported your father. I have been a victim just like anyone else, he never treated me like a wife nor did he care for his daughter. Why should you kill us for his sins . . . why? Why? Why?" (She sobbed hysterically) . . . Hokoyo with quick deft movements grabbed the woman, stood her up and gave her a back hander with all his weight which drew blood on the woman's mouth and sent her reeling backwards.

"The Commander's family was just as innocent – you filthy bitch! Why didn't you persuade your evil husband to slow down on his sell-out schemes? Throughout the war we had snakes like you throwing spanners in our strategies – selling us out to Rhodesian forces" Turning to Kuda:

"Chief, can I go ahead and take this bunch to the bushes over there and get done with them? Hokoyo asked drooling at the thought of who knows what – but his eyes and grin showed that mercy was not in his vocabulary and believe me being on the wrong side of him was enough torture. But Kuda ignored him and went on with a sneer . . .

"Woman! My families was just as innocent but were killed; so, anything or anyone that has been and is an associate with these two men should be punished and the only punishment is death just like he did with an uncountable families here at the Stud"

Shungu himself had been hoping for a chance to avenge his family's savage killings but watching Hokoyo and imagining what he would do to Sarah before killing her for something that she was just as much a victim simply because of being Spinach's daughter was more than he could bear. But here was his long lost brother seething with a deep sited hate and a choking thirst for vengeance. The love of his life Sarah, a woman he loved so dearly staked to be brutally slain by his own brother – NO! He decided; if Sarah was to die, then he must die too. He shouted nervously . . .

"Wait! – Kuda, I beg you to listen to what I have to say. I know how much you and I both suffered because of Spinach and Stewart and I know the pain we both feel to this day, but a lot have happened since you left. I have never been able to forgive these two (pointing) and will never forgive them. But to begrudge their wives and children is going a bit too far" Turning to the crowd Shungu went on . . .

"Why should you punish his wife and daughter? What did they do wrong; Spinach must suffer for his evil deeds which you all know did not need any influence from anyone but himself. Besides why should you want to have Spinach's blood on your hands; he is old and will soon die anywhere, and, the blood of all the people he had killed will haunt him for the rest of his life right through to his grave which from the looks of it is not long. Right now, the most important issue is to see change in our working conditions, have better accommodation, better wages and a good Foreman" Shungu explained mainly for Sarah's sake.

"Shungu, you seem to be forgetting something – Our parents are dead because of these men. I believe in a sword for a sword and to grant my father's last wish" Kuda retorted with a surprise look.

"No Brother! For the past years, I have felt the same way, but seeing you here as Commander, and remembering how we survived made me realize that our family flag still stands up high and Spinach's life is as good as dead, and look at Stewart, he's already a moving grave. As far as I'm concerned our parents have avenged in their own way. Also look at all these people, if you get rid of the farm owners, all these people will have no jobs, no wages and no place to stay; surely freedom does not mean making your own people suffer because that is what will happen to all these families" Shungu persisted. Kuda paced up and down with one hand on his waist and the other stroking his beard thoughtfully – whilst his brother looked on eagerly.

"I must say your stay with Father James has made you into a weakling, I cannot imagine you begging for these cruel people's lives after watching our parents gunned down like wild pigs. Actually you are right I will not kill them but I'm sure the wild animals will do the honors that way they will die a brutal death and suffer the same way they made families suffer" Turning to look at his two bodyguards Kuda ordered . . .

"Shumba and Hokoyo take these three men (pointing at Spinach, Sidney and Stewart) in the thickest part of the forest with plenty wild animals especially around Whirl-shire area; make sure it is more than 50 miles away from society. Drop them off with no water or food I understand the Lions in that area are desperate for softer prey – we will deal with the rest of their families". Stewart who had fainted and had long since come round but was still sprawled in the grit pretending to be in a comma whilst listening and catching on to every word spoken between the brothers hoping Shungu would put in a word for him and his son realized his fantasy was over when he heard the gruesome order – his eyes snapped wide open and he scrambled onto his feet. He had to face the truth about the situation. The game was over for him – Shungu's brother was sick, mentally deranged and for the first time he was truly scared. Stewart started screaming for his son to shoot him than to be eaten by wild animals. His whole body was shaking. Spinach unable to stand crawled to Hokoyo's feet begging for mercy but instead got a big hard kick that sent him rolling. Sidney knowing if there was hope it would be from Shungu – with fear written all over his face he begged for his life . . .

"Shungu, please talk to your brother into sparing our lives I will give you one million dollars, please – do something". Shungu looked straight in Sidney's eyes . . . .

"In case you have forgotten what you were trying to do to me – I have a good mind of telling my brother about it, which will make your situation much worse than it already is; besides you already owe everyone on this farm much more than that for all the years of cheap labor and inhuman treatment especially from your father" Shungu responded angrily. That made Sidney turn red with fear and panic.

Sarah tagged at Shungu's shirt; he turned and met the sadness and pity in her big brown eyes . . .

"Stop him, Shungu please" she whispered. Sarah hated her father but seeing him lying there helplessly thawed all the anger in her and was replaced by love for a father. She thought of all kinds of reasons why he acted the way he did blaming herself in the process – she was torn between love for a father she barely knew and a man she loved whole-heartedly. She was not worried about herself because she felt that if she was not going to be with Shungu life was not worth living anywhere. The look in her eyes pierced Shungu's heart so much that without thinking he strode towards Hokoyo and met him halfway firmly blocking his way . . .

"I can't let you do this – no I can't" Shungu said standing his ground. Hokoyo had to battle with a strong urge within to strangle the Commander's brother – instead he spun and looked at Kuda as if to say tell this fool to get out of my way.

"What the hell are you doing Shungu? Don't test my patience you hear? These idiots mercilessly murdered our parents for heaven's sake!" Garikayi blared angrily

"I know! But what good will it do to kill them? I don't want my only brother to have the blood of a bunch of pagans on his hands. Shungu stammered . . .

"Damn!" Kuda swore. He punched a big fist into the palm of his hand and walked up to his brother grinding his teeth. Everyone stood rigidly and completely still, a deafening silence blanketed the air around as the brothers bore into each other's eyes. Shungu was rattling from fear within but somehow managed to keep a cool head.

"I'm sorry Kuda the brutal murder of our family was the first and the last of killings I will see. You said it yourself freedom is not about revenge – remember what Father James taught us? You fought for freedom and freedom is here – Are you going to kill every farmer or white man and every sell-out you see? Don't you see that you as a Commander if you start avenging, others will follow the same example and there will be no control or order in the Country? Look at Stewart right now, the embarrassment of being in the situation he's in right now is enough to kill him without you lifting a finger on him. As your brother I beg you to listen to me just this once." He begged. All eyes and ears were on the two brothers. Kuda in the while was looking at Stewart and Spinach with an expressionless face but his eyes were menacing. After a long pause that felt like a lifetime Kuda turned to his brother again and in a curious abrupt voice – he asked . . . .

"Shungu can you tell me your real reason for wanting these evil lives to be spared? I feel there's more to it than you are actually saying" Shungu hesitated for a few seconds not sure if it was the right time to talk about Sarah. On impulse he looked at her as if wanting assurance. Kuda followed his gaze and before Shungu could say anything asked . . .

"Who's that girl?" pointing. Everyone's gaze moved from the brothers to Sarah including her parents. She felt so embarrassed that she wished the ground would just open and swallow her. Her legs were giving in but Shungu's love gave her strength; when she looked at him no one else mattered not even her own life. Shungu beckoned her to come where he was but it seemed as if her feet were stuck to the ground because she didn't move. He walked to her and holding her hand led her to where Kuda was standing . . . 'She is a brunette, all she needs is proper dressing and that beauty would flare up' Kuda thought.

"This is Sarah . . . she . . . she's . . . mmmm . . . ." Shungu hesitated

"Shungu what has become of you?" You're even finding a simple introduction to your girlfriend hard; even a fool can tell you are both in love because of the way you look at each other so what's the big deal?" Kuda chuckled and went on: I must say she is quite a knock out, I don't blame you for falling head over heal in love with her." (If you think the news of Shungu and Kuda being Nhamo's children was a shocker; this brought an even bigger reaction except for Sarah, Sidney and Shungu's Auntie and her husband because everyone thought Shungu was Sidney's lover. That piece of news broke the silence. But only for a minute or so because no one wanted to miss anything. The gravy had thickened everyone that knew that Sarah was Spinach's daughter was waiting to see Kuda's reaction to that piece of the puzzle that he didn't know yet. Spinach that had very little care for his daughter suddenly had some strength and hopes that being Sarah's father might be spared as the future 'father in law'. Sarah's mother was shocked to think that her daughter of all people attracted the educated boy Shungu. She looked at her daughter with so much pride and other women where looking at her with envy.

"So! You are the girl that has turned my brother's heart into a marshmallow? Well I'm sure you have lived here longer than him; can you help me to make him see sense regarding Stewart and Spinach?" Before Sarah could say anything Mheni who had overheard the women standing next to him talking shouted out . . .

"Chief! That is Spinach's daughter" Kuda asked Mheni to repeat what he had just said because he thought he did not hear right the first time. He looked sharply at Shungu, to Sarah and back to Shungu with his mouth open and a questioning expression on his face. The smile that had formed on his face disappeared so fast and was replaced by unmistakable rage . . .

"What! SPINACH's daughter HELL NO! (He snapped) Oh no brother, there's no way – do you realize that she will be a constant reminder of what her father did to our family – how can you live with that? No way! I'm taking you to the Capital and there you will meet more beauties than you care to count, educated with a lot of talent. This is the most absurd relationship. I will not stand here and watch you make a fool of yourself – of all girls to pick on a viper's viper?" He asked with a sudden cold dislike for Sarah . . .

"Kuda, I understand what you are saying, but I want you to know that Sarah is part of my life now and without her I've nothing to live for. Do not hate her because of her father; she was as much a victim as anyone of us here. Besides I didn't know that she was Spinach's daughter until much later, and when I did I had to ask Auntie for her opinion because I didn't know what to do, but they assured me that Sarah was a nice sweet girl who respected everyone – something that I have also proved. Like you said – of all girls why did our ancestors lead me to her? I hate to say this but she either comes with me or I stay here on the farm" Shungu said firmly looking directly at Kuda.

"Listen Shungu, the Chief is right, you have not seen any part of the Country besides the closed walls of this farm. Why don't you come with us and survey then come back for her when you have settled down" Hokoyo chipped in trying to make Shungu see what he (Hokoyo) thought was sense. There was silence. Kuda looked at his brother but his thoughts seemed to be far away like someone deep in thought, he lit a cigarette inhaled a lung full pacing in semi-circles, all eyes following his every step.

Suddenly two thin tall figures stood before him, their rugged clothes barely covering the worn out bodies. The feet covered in mud and no doubt never knew the feel of shoes. They seemed to fear him because they thought he would blame them for encouraging Shungu to fall in love with Sarah and were not sure if he would want them to touch his crispy clean uniform. Looking at them Kuda immediately knew that it was his Aunt and her husband and could sense the fear in them. Without saying a word he pulled them both to him and wrapped his arms around them. His Aunt who was already sobbing started wailing. Kuda realizing his uniform was getting wet with tears and mucus slowly untangles himself from them and as if remembering something – thrust his hand in his pocket and pulled out a letter, he handed it to his Uncle. It was a letter from their Son asking them to come and join him in Salisbury where he was living with his wife and a daughter. The excitement of knowing their son was alive and well wiped out all the fear and tears of pure joy came streaking out in huge sobs. Kuda asked them to go and pack their belongings because he was going to take them to their son. As if wanting more time to absorb the news of Shungu and Sarah, Kuda called his assistant and started a tête-à-tête. After a good 30 minutes of shifting his weight from one foot to another he walked slowly toward the Rover opened the door and sat with his legs hanging out and puffing smoke from his fifth cigarette. Hokoyo joined him.

Hokoyo was a stout heavily built man with a clean – head. He was given the nickname Hokoyo (watch-out) because of his 'act first and talk later attitude'. He hardly smiled and when he did he looked like he was crying. He rarely laughed loud except a grin, sneer or a chuckle. Killing to him was like breaking an egg in a frying pan – no one dared to cross his path. He voluntarily joined the war after a man in their village went and told the soldiers that some people in his village were feeding freedom fighters and soldiers raided the village where he lived. Men including his father were tortured for information about the whereabouts of the (freedom fighters) gorillas as they were called. His father's fingers were cut off during torture and his mother was forced to eat them before they were brutally killed. His sister was taken away and later found raped and her throat slit. Hokoyo survived because he was out hunting with five other boys his age. On arrival they saw the soldiers; the other boys ran into the bush, he climbed a tree and hid in the branches – from there he watched people being tortured and killed then the whole village was burnt down. When the soldiers finally left the few that had managed to escape came back. Together they dug a mass grave and buried their dead. A month after the massacre the gorillas' came-by in transit and him being 19 years old begged to join them. Kuda was in charge of the troop and he gladly agreed. To him sell-outs like Spinach did not deserve mercy; neither did the brutal killer like Stewart.

During their conversation Hokoyo convinced Kuda that he should go along with his brother's wish not to kill the two then later he (Hokoyo) would come back and get rid of them without Shungu knowing and he also told him that he can let Sarah go with Shungu but will meet with an accident in Salisbury when Shungu was not around. To Kuda that certainly sounded like a good plan and knowing Hokoyo he knew it was just a matter of time. He began to thaw and the stiffness that he had begun to feel went away. He put weight back on his feet and walked slowly and carelessly back to Shungu looking blankly at him and hunching his shoulders. In almost a whisper he said:

"You are my kid brother and nothing can change that, if this is what you want I will not stand in your way. But I want you to know that SHE (pointing at Sarah) will never be welcome at my house as long as I'm still alive. Sarah who had been holding back tears began to cry. Since no one had heard what Kuda said they thought Sarah was crying because her father was going to be killed. Kuda started pacing again this time with his .38 pistol in hand and looking at the gun as if he was seeing it for the first time. Again, there was unbearable silence, coughs were suppressed and babies suckled to sleep or just silenced by the udder. Spinach was sitting like a rabbit cornered by a fox. Even Shungu for that moment was afraid of his brother but he stood his ground to see what would happen next.

"My father needs medical attention, his gasping for air" Sidney screamed to no one in particular and breaking the silence. There was a gunshot from Kuda and the bullet landed right between Juan's parted feet. That silenced him faster than a turned off radio. Spinach screamed and his bowels loosened. Anyone close to him had to move because of the smell. Everyone thought the first shot was a miss and a massacre was about to take place, some sympathized but some thought 'an eye for an eye'. 'Blood is certainly thicker than water' Hokoyo thought, because he had never seen his boss hesitate or change his decisions and of all people Kuda was the only person he was afraid of because he knew that behind that musk was a ruthless man that knew no boundaries but, seeing him hesitate and even give thought to his brother's plea – a person that has never fought the war and does not know the hardships, pain, and torture that he (Hokoyo) and others experienced in the hands of the Smith Regime made him sick to his stomach. To Hokoyo the more bodies he counted the better he felt. He was ready to kill this very minute and the thought gave him pleasure that he grinned. As if reading his mind Kuda ordered him to back off. Which he did with a very slow pace and eyes probing right through the three figures as if to say your days are numbered.

"You better thank my kid brother who has a heart of a woman but remember Hokoyo's face because you will see it again" Kuda said in a raspy voice and still holding his gun.

Shungu wanting to make sure everyone understood why he did what he did; he walked and stood by his brother's side . . .

"Our opinion might differ but that does not mean I have no respect for my brother Kuda" he said and went on . . . "I know how he feels towards these people because I know the pain we both suffered watching our parents and sisters killed. But sometimes we need to let go of the past and look to the future. I will never forgive Spinach and Stewart for what they did but what will killing them bring to us; my family and some of your families are gone and will never come back no matter what we do now. Some of you might think I am doing this because of Sarah but if that was the case why would I bother about Stewart? He has no relationship with her. Let's bury the hatches and look to building our Country together and making sure our children do not grow up in a similar situation or condition. Stewart needs to compensate each and everyone's relative that he killed and he can only do that alive than dead" Shungu concluded giving his brother a pat on the shoulder. One old man stood up and started clapping in acknowledgement, then another, then another before long almost half had stood up but others did not agree with him but where afraid to argue so they just kept sitting watching Kuda's reaction. Unfortunately there was none he only shook his head and threw his hand in the air as if in surrender. He beckoned to Hokoyo to take the floor with the instructions he had given him. As he passed by Stewart he paused and through clenched teeth he said:

"I want you to listen to what Mheni is going to say and you better listen very carefully. Know that your every move is being watched – just as you had your filthy spy Spinach so will I have mine watching your every move and one mistake you won't know how you got to devil's door – a door you'll gladly knock because living will just be as unbearable." He took a step and holding his pistol and put it on Sidney's head and before anyone could say anything he pulled the trigger. Sidney sprawled to the ground with a deafening scream; Stewart tried to scream but was only able to squeak his eyes wide open in horror. Spinach was shaking like someone suffering from Malaria – his face ashen with fear written all over it. Women screamed causing babies to start crying. Everyone was taken aback by the sudden event but when Kuda and his men burst out laughing everyone realized the gun was not loaded making most men join in the laughter including Shungu and Sarah.

CHAPTER EIGHT

THE ARRIVAL OF Kuda and his men changed many things at the Seven Stud. Stewart's wife and his older son had been summoned and were present. But before long Stewart, whose condition had deteriorated – was driven away to the hospital by his wife with the help of Shungu's persistence. Mheni, who was from the Labor office stipulated the rules and assured Sidney and his brother that he would be back to check that everything that he had said was being followed. Spinach was pruned of his position and therefore was no longer a Foreman; he was demoted to working the fields like everyone else. His house was to be given to the new foreman appointed by the workers which meant Spinach would need to build his own poll and dagger thatched hut. A worker's committee that consisted of seven members was formed. Sidney was asked to start looking into improving the workers living conditions and a minimum wage was set. He went on to explain to the workers what the duties of the Committee were, and then added:

"I need to point out that, independence does not mean you stop working, the manager will keep an eye on you, to make sure you are doing your work. Anyone found not doing what they are supposed to do – with the help of the committee, will be fired. The manager will report to the Committee, the Committee will report to the owner and he will report to our office and if need be, we will give him the authority to fire anyone found breaking the law. We need a prosperous law binding Country and need to set a good example to our neighboring countries that are still fighting for freedom about what freedom is all about. As for those that need to go to school, let it be known that schools will be open to the public very soon". The last remark brought such joy that for a while all you could here were voices in a cloud of dust.

Sidney was asked to offer one of his beasts for the celebrations, which lasted well into the early hours of the following day. For the first time in history people were able to talk freely without worrying about who was listening. The African brew, which was brewed privately, was drunk openly. Kuda and his men had come with crates and crates of English beer, which none of the peasant including Shungu had ever tasted since it was illegal for any black person to be found drinking clear bear. This day everyone at the Stud had a taste of it. Sidney and his brother were forced to stick around during most of the ceremony.

Word of what had happened at the Stud spread to the neighboring farms like an inferno. Some farmers, not sure of their fate and knowing the suppressed anger in the laborers packed and fled whilst their works were in the fields. One unfortunate farmer and his wife were attacked and killed by the workers after they tried to stop them from celebrating freedom. Their three children survived because the quick thinking maid ran into the house grabbed the children and ran with them into the bush before anyone noticed. It is said she walked for nearly 4 miles before she came across another fleeing white couple and seeing the white children stopped and gave them a ride together with the maid. They made a report to the nearest police station that immediately came to the farm and found the farmhouse ransacked and most of the property vandalized. The actions of the workers on this particular farm were later described as barbaric and shallow mindedness. Arrests were made and the couple's bodies were taken away by the police.

Sidney's mind was busy planning what to do as soon as Kuda and his men left because he knew the farm was no longer a safe place to stay – not with all he had done to some of the men not to mention his father. He decided he would sell the farm and move to South Africa where he knew he would still have the power since the Country was still under white rule and apartheid was on the rampage. His brother already lived in the City (Whirl-shire) close to his Wine factory and five star Hotel that he owned and his parents would live in one of the properties they owned in the Capital City Salisbury. These thoughts pleased him. As he watched the dancing that was going on, his gaze fixed on Shungu who had his back on him. Sidney started fantasizing and building castles with Shungu as his partner. His brother looked at him and saw him drooling and knew exactly what he was thinking . . .

"Knock it off! Dad has been taken to the hospital and we don't know his condition and here we are not knowing our fate and you have the cheek to think of sex? What's wrong with you?" His brother whispered angrily.

"You have your life I have mine" Sidney retorted still looking at Shungu. As if sensing that someone was watching him Shungu turned just to in time to see the look that he recognized each time he had an encounter with Sidney. Not able to stand it he asked his brother if they could be allowed to leave since Mheni had said all he wanted them to hear. Hokoyo did not waste time . . .

"You two (pointing to Sidney and his brother) are excused – go and start planning the changes as stipulated and remember – you are being watched" he said with a threat in his voice. Sidney's brother did not hear half what Hokoyo said except the word 'GO' they both scrambled to their feet and half trotted and half ran towards their mansion. Suddenly there was a gunshot; the brothers froze in their tracks; the bullet brushed Sidney's hair leaving a trim just above the ear, there was a short silence as everyone was trying to figure out what was happening. Then a queer hysterical laughter came from Hokoyo who was enjoying every minute of it . . .

"That is a warning of what is to come if you do not comply – don't ever think I missed, that was deliberate" he shouted to the brothers who were ways away. No sooner had Hokoyo turned his back the brothers ran as fast as their legs could go because they knew that man was as ruthless as he looked and could snap at anytime. Once indoors they felt secure. Sidney explained his plans to his brother who agreed fully with the decision to leave. Sidney was on the phone to the accountant whilst his brother called the hospital to find out his father's condition and briefly explaining to his mother what they had decided to do. Not wanting to waste time they started parking their personal belongings – there was a knock on the door.

SPINACH had sneaked away from the celebrations and followed Sidney to the house hoping he could work something out with them. He waited whilst Sidney was on the phone then tapped on the door quietly. Sidney not sure who was knocking grabbed his pistol and in a quivering voice asked

"Who is it?"

"Spinach, Bass!" he said also quivering. For a spit second Sidney was worried thinking Spinach must have heard his intentions to sell the property. Then he remembered that Spinach couldn't speak or understand English except 'chilapalapa' (a mixture of English and Shona words that was used by most Whites to communicate)

"What do you want? He barked. Have you not caused enough trouble? My father is seriously ill in hospital therefore does not need your services anymore and I for one have never and will never need your services, so, get going before I give you a free ticket to HELL" he shouted without opening the door.

Spinach immediately knew that he had been used and had never been Stewart's favorite but his tool. He looked around in confusion and felt his whole life curving in. Suddenly he started running as if demon possessed (in his old age it was more like trotting). He got to the tool shed grabbed a rope to hang himself on one of the trees in the cornfield. He climbed the tree tied a knot but could not find the guts to take his life.

It was just before mid-night when Kuda and his men decided to leave. The officer (Mheni) was staying behind for a few days to help the committee with the rules and regulations and would stay in the cabin where Shungu was staying. Shungu's Uncle and his wife were already sitting in the truck with all their belongings, which barely filled a 10 ream box. SARAH clever as she was noticed the sudden change in Kuda's attitude after talking to Hokoyo and also noticed the cold icy eye she kept getting from Hokoyo. She immediately knew that they were up to something. As much as she loved Shungu she decided she would not risk her life by going to Salisbury. It was not easy to convince Shungu to leave her behind but she finally did. Shungu promised to keep in touch and be back as soon as he got a job and a place of his own. Kuda did not really want to have to live with the guilty of Sarah's death so her decision not to come with them was a thrill for him. He did not worry about Shungu because he thought it was just a matter of introducing him to the Salisbury girls and he would forget about the peasant girl. Hokoyo was already planning how to get rid of Stewart and Spinach, which to him was anytime soon. As they drove away the farm workers chanted slogans, sang and danced around the truck for a good mile as it drove away honking loudly until it was out of sight. Shungu hardly spoke during the drive to Salisbury. His mind kept drifting back to Sarah's sweet innocent face and could not believe that he let her convince him into leaving her even though it was based on him having to get a job and a place of his own first. He felt like he had left part of his heart behind. He vowed that as soon as he got a job and a place of his own, he would come back for Sarah – THAT WAS BEFORE HE SAW THE BRIGHT LIGHTS OF SALISBURY.

On arrival in Salisbury Shungu's eyes were almost popping out of their sockets in wonderment. When he walked into Kuda's house he rubbed his eyes over and over again hoping to wake up from the unbelievable dream. The five roomed house to him looked like a queen's palace he had once seen in one of the magazines that he saw whilst in school and to imagine the house was owned by his brother was a story that only belonged to dreams. When he saw what was to be his bedroom he was very convinced it was all but a dream, he looked more like a kid in a toy store. His mouth was just as wide as his eyes. A house fly thought it had found its self a new home when it flew right past the lips into the open mouth. He nearly choked on in but was able to spit it out. That brought a loud laugh from Hokoyo that no one had ever seen or heard, he rolled to the floor, tapping his thigh with his left hand and everyone else joined in except Shungu who didn't find it funny.

There was no question that this was a raw African from the bundus (deep down) of the African jungle and it was so obvious that his every move portrayed his ignorance. He was fascinated by anything from a shower, stove, street lights, telephone – anything, name it and it thrilled him. But in it all he kept wishing Sarah would be there to share this amazing side of the world with him. When he wrote the first letter to Sarah, it was all about how he longed to have her by his side and describing all the wonders he was seeing day by day. He did not trust his brother to mail the letter so he asked the maid to mail it. As days turned to weeks and weeks to months, he began to act like a snake that had just pulled off its old skin. He was adjusting very well and was no longer acting weird.

Kuda decided it was time to introduce him to a new topic that would definitely change him mentally and physically – women! Kuda who was a womanizer himself decided to set up a blind date for Shungu with one of the ladies from his office and this was in hope that Shungu would forget about Sarah whom he knew his brother was still communicating with. Kuda knew that if he asked Shungu to meet the girl he would refuse so he asked his girlfriend Loyce to bring along Emma who already knew what the scoop was. The meeting place was a five star hotel called Meikles. It was one of the best hotels in the City and was very popular to most top foreign delegates and tourists. The four met in the foyer:

"This is my girlfriend Loyce and Loyce, this is my brother Shungu" Kuda introduced. Shungu raised his eyebrows in surprise because the girlfriend he knew was Charity but he let it slid and extended his hand to greet Loyce. "And you are?" he asked extending his hand to greet the other woman. "My name is Emma" she said smiling exposing a set of milky white teeth which seemed to blend in perfectly with big brown watery eyes perched squarely above a sharp but small nose. They headed to the swing and sway hall where a local band was playing. Shungu needed very little convincing because Emma was a clear cut knock out and she knew how to manipulate men and they always fell in like cows being dipped in debar (a pool with chemicals to kill ticks). By the end of the night he was hooked like a tiger fish and all resistance sucked out. In the months that followed the communication with Sarah became less and less until Sarah was non-existence. The last letter he wrote to her said:

"Thank you for the times we shared Sarah. I really miss the moments. But a man must move on. I cannot bear the distance and the class difference that is now there between us. So I found someone to match my current status in life. I am planning on getting married to the most beautiful woman, and I'd advise that you find yourself a nice guy to settle down with. Don't bother to write me because I have moved to a new address which I deliberately excluded in this correspondence. I'm sorry but such is life.

Shungu.

Kuda had won all round because without Shungu's knowledge they had gone back to the Seven Stud and they found that the farm was under new management and the name had changed. Stewart did not survive his heart attack, Spinach had committed suicide, Sidney and his mother had moved to South Africa but the brother was still running his businesses and living in Whirlshire. Sarah's mother was still living and working on the farm but they did not see Sarah and no one told them her whereabouts. That did not bother Kuda because he thought after not hearing from Shungu she must have gone and got married.

Seven years had passed since Shungu arrived in Salisbury now Harare and the Country's name had changed from Rhodesia to Zimbabwe. Kuda had landed him a job in the Ministry of Tourism. He worked during the day and went to school in the evening and that helped him to be promoted to a better position that offered accommodation and a company car. Unable to contain his love for Emma he decided to ask for her hand in marriage, and she gladly agreed. He was so excited and not wanting to waste time decided to notify his Auntie who was now living like a queen with her son, daughter-in-law and grand children. Unfortunately, her husband had died from Malaria barely a year after they arrived in Harare.

When Shungu arrived at Nhau's house with Emma on his heels, he saw his Auntie sitting under a jacaranda tree busy inhaling her favorite snuff. Signs of old age were now evident. Her hearing was no longer as good and her sight was just as bad. Shungu sneaked up on her and grabbed the snuff packet from her in a teasing manner:

"Nhau, I don't like these games of yours – do you hear" she quivered pointing to no one in particular with a hand that shook from her Parkinson disease.

"It's me Auntie! I brought you two more packets of your favorite snuff" Shungu said laughing.

"Oh Kuda, it's you! How is Rute . . . ." "I am Rutendo, now I am convinced you need to see a doctor about your eyes" Shungu said seriously.

"Doctors are for your kids I am just waiting for my good Lord to take me to a place where my husband is waiting for me and I hope it is soon because I am ready" she responded sadly.

"Anywhere, I have come to introduce the woman I have decided to marry, her nam . . ." Shungu was explaining but was interrupted.

"About time son, I was worried that you were going to lose Sarah and besides I don't need any introduction I saw the girl from birth, this is the best decision you hav . . ."

"Auntie, this is Emma. I left Sarah a long time ago and I'm sure she is married by now" Shungu interrupted surprised that she was still thinking of Sarah.

"Are you crazy? Leaving a sweat girl like Sarah for these prostitutes of Harare? If it's a blessing you are looking for, it won't come from me – and to think I thought you were the intelligent of my sister's two boys. I am glad she is not here to see this nonsense" she said spitting on her reed mat.

"How can you say that, you don't even know the girl?" Shungu said suppressing the urge to scream at her.

"Nhau once came with a friend that introduced his girlfriend as Eeem; I am sure she is the same one – it's a wonder how you kids don't get venereal desea . . ." she was interrupted by Nhau's wife who came out of the house after hearing voices outside.

"Oh my, look at what the cat has dragged in; what has been keeping you busy that you forget about us or shall I say your Auntie? The last time we saw you was at the funeral – how are you doing?" She said hugging Shungu and not waiting for him to respond she turned to the woman next to Shungu and said:

"Hi Emma, this is an even bigger surprise – how is Jonathan?" she said extending her hand in greeting.

"You know each other? Shungu asked puzzled.

"Oh yeah! She is Jonathan's girlfriend" She responded without a thought

"Was!" Not anymore, I love Shungu. Emma said angrily.

"Am I missing something here?" Nhau's wife asked

"I told you so, I told you so" turning to her daughter-in-law "this is the woman Shungu has come to introduce to soon be his wife – can you believe that?"

"What?" Wait until Nhau hears about this" she said walking back into the house and closing the door behind her. Shungu felt embarrassed, shocked and angry. He held his Auntie's hand and simply said:

"You still have it in you – the sixth sense. I will see you later, Auntie"

"Don't say I didn't warn you" she called out.

Emma tried to explain but Shungu was not ready for any explanation. He just wanted to get home and think everything through after dropping Emma at her house. When he got to his house there was a message waiting for him from Kuda's new girlfriend Gertrude. The message was that Kuda had been taken away to the hospital after suddenly collapsing in his living room. Frantically, he got back in the car and drove to the hospital, all thoughts of Emma and everything that had happened wiped out. His heart racing, he got to the hospital and in no time he was standing by Kuda's bedside. He was in the intensive care unit. The nurse was busy connecting all kinds of machines that Shungu did not know:

"Nurse, is he going to be okay? What is wrong with him? Is he . . ." He went on not giving the nurse a chance to answer until she cut him short . . .

"Calm down, he needs all the support he can get right now, the Doctor has taken all the tests and she will be here later with the results. Are you a relative?"

"Yes, I am his brother." He responded very concerned.

"Well, as you can see the signs are not good, but the doctor will fill you in since you are a relative. I will be leaving shortly and the nurse on night shift will be able to assist you with any questions. But for now you need to go and wait in the waiting room" She explained. Shungu walked out feeling a huge lump on his throat, he felt like everything was tumbling down around him. In all the years after leaving the orphanage he had not thought of God and right now he felt he needed God more than ever. Suddenly, he began to pray with his face in the palm of his hands. The prayer was cut short by a tap on his shoulder:

"Are you Shungu? The Doctor asked.

"Yes I am. Is my brother going to be okay?

"Come to my office" he said leading him to the office a few doors away from where Kuda was. He closed the door behind him and said:

"You need to be strong for your brother; he is going to need all the support he can get (paused) he has AIDS and the disease in incurable. We can only stabilize him but there is no cure and here in the third world we do not have the actual medication to help the immune deficiency. The longest he might survive is six months because his CD count is below 20 and the viral load is in thousands – I am sorry" Shungu cried uncontrollably, the Doctor hopeless in the situation just held his hand and let him cry. When he finally calmed down the Doctor told him to go and see his brother who had finally opened his eyes and was being attended to by the night-shift nurse. Shungu not wanting Kuda to know that he had been crying rubbed his eyes with his shirt before opening the door to the ward. When Shungu opened the door the nurse was busy taking Kuda's blood pressure. Two steps into the room, the nurse turned and before him was Sarah. Shungu froze in his tracks, his heart was racing so fast he thought he was going to faint he could not believe that this gorgeous woman standing before him was once his one and only and to imagine that he threw it all away – and for what? He thought. He took a few more steps towards Sarah:

"Oh my God, Sarah, is it you" he said, but her voice made him step back:

"Don't you dare come close. You chose to toss me like a rug because you saw nothing in me besides some uneducated peasant smelling of dung but guess what; there is a God. She pushed him aside and stepped out banging the door behind her. Shungu slowly pulled a chair and virtually threw himself in it:

"How could I be so stupid to let go of a jewel that my ancestors had placed in my arms and go for some cheap floozy like Emma. I accepted to be influenced by Kuda and his ferocious style so much that I got blinded to the love of my life. I need her back in my life; I need her, I nee . . ."

"Shungu are you okay?" Kuda asked in a weak voice. He did not recognize Sarah and he did not hear the brief conversation between the nurse and his brother.

Shungu got up slowly and stood before his brother. One mind wanted to hate him for making him lose Sarah but like they say, blood is thicker than water. He held Kuda's hand and promised him that he would take care of him just like they did from the day their parents died. He went on to tell him that the nurse who was taking care of him was the same Sarah he hated and now here she was treating him. Kuda even though sick could sense the emotion in Shungu's voice and knowing he playing a bigger role in separating them began to cry silently.

"I want to confess that I set up the arrangement for you to meet with Emma because I hated Spinach's daughter and worse of all I am remorseful for trapping you with a woman that I knew was a prostitute. I hope you find room in your heart to forgive me." He said through sobs.

"There is nothing to forgive, I was the weak one because all you did was bring me to the water but it was my decision to drink it and so I cannot blame you. All I can do now is to try and figure out how to win her back, if at all" Shungu said sadly. He waited in hope that Sarah would come back but she didn't so he finally left intending to come back the following evening when he knew she would be on shift.

⸻⸻⸻

Sarah had not recognized Kuda because he had lost so much weight due to his illness; it was only after she saw Shungu that she realized who her patient was. Her heart was pounding heavy blows to her chest when she saw Shungu, she was so angry but deep down she knew she still loved him – how could she not . . . this was the man who fathered her son and daughter (twins). After walking out she asked her co-worker to take over the shift because she was not feeling well. By the time she got to her car she was already sobbing.

When Shungu left for Salisbury, (now called Harare) the passionate kisses before his departure, his promise that he'd come back for her, and how they were going to get married, how she so very much believed him, all added up to create a lump in her throat, as all the memories came tumbling back. Sarah only discovered that she was pregnant, three weeks after his departure. Through the hand of God, she managed to get a job as a cleaner at the rural district council clinic. She worked half time and in the afternoon would attend classes. She was preparing herself so that she would easily blend in with City life when Shungu returned to get her. She kept the pregnancy a secret because she did not want him to rush back without completing his plans according to the letters he was writing. The matron of the clinic liked Sarah because of her hard-work and so seeing that in her state going to and from the farm that was four miles away was too much for her, decided to offer her a room in one of the cottages by the clinic. She had to share with three other women but she didn't care because her eyes were on the prize – her goals. She grabbed this opportunity with both hands. What bothered her most was the fact that Shungu had ceased all forms of communication with her. She had received five letters in the first two months after his departure; the letters were full of the usual "I Love you-" blah-blah's, followed by sudden silence from him. At first, she would cry herself to sleep from missing him, confused, unable to understand why he would cease to keep her posted on his progress and plans. All her plans came to naught. What she in fact received from Shungu, a year and five months after his departure, was a letter, telling her to forget him. Sarah was devastated, but the revelation came as no surprise. For the nine months she carried his child (she didn't know it was a set of twins) and the torturous labor pains she endured before giving birth to the two babies had hardened her resolve. She had endured enough single handedly to bother about the letter and wondered why he even bothered to write her. The fact that he did meant that he purposely wanted to hurt her feelings, or worse, drive her into committing suicide. At that particular stage, Sarah was performing miracles in her studies whilst her mother took care of her children. She had come out with straight "A"s at advanced level, majoring in the toughest of combinations-Math, Physics, and Chemistry. She went from a cleaner to a nurse aid at the clinic. She continued with her studies to become a nurse and when she completed her course she became a full time nurse at the clinic where she made a good name for herself as a good hearted, generous and hardworking nurse with a big heart for the sick. Five years later, there was an opening at Harare Central Hospital. The matron asked her to apply for the position and as luck would have it she got the job after a very good reference from the matron. She first moved to Harare on her own, leaving her children with her mother but without fail sending money, clothes and food every single month. When she finally found a house and school for her kids, she went back to the farm and moved her mother and children to Harare. In the two years that she had worked at Harare Central Hospital she had bought herself a second hand car and was living a life that one would call middle class and she was contented. So many men had tried to court her but she kept turning them down. She devoted her life to her children and her job. Now here she was face to face with Shungu. In the last letter that he wrote he said he was getting married so the two of them ever getting together was no longer possible (she thought) but her worry was about the children, how would he react if she told him about them. When she finally went back to work Shungu had left.

Shungu asked the receptionist what time nurses on night shift knocked off and was told at 7:00 AM and he also found out that being Friday they would be off duty for three days. So not wanting to wait for another three days to see Sarah, he decided to come back first thing in the morning and wait outside by the main entrance. He sat in his car from 6:30 AM and a few minutes after seven he saw Sarah walk out with two other nurses. They parted ways as she headed to the car. She started the car and as she maneuvered out of the parking lot, Shungu followed.

She did not pay attention to the car following behind because she was so engrossed with thoughts of what had happened.

'I know that as long as Kuda is still in hospital Shungu will be back so how do I avoid him? I cannot believe that after all he did to me I still love him – God made it plan clear that I would not forget him by giving me a son with all features of his father. If I tell my children that I saw your father, they will insist on seeing him especially Benjamin who has been bugging me since we first arrived in Harare – how do I tell them that their father has a family of his own and did not want to see them.' The last thought brought her to tears. As she neared the gate to the house she was renting in one of the high-density surbarbs her son Benjamin was already there to open the gate. She quickly rubbed off the tears and gave a forced smile as she drove past him. She quickly got out of the car and with quick steps headed for the house:

"Mum! Wait for me" Benjamin called out from the gate that he was struggling to close. Shungu who had just slowed down slightly passed the gate heard the boy call Sarah 'Mum'. His heart sank and all hopes of getting back together with Sarah wiped out:

'It did not even occur to me that after all these years she could have got married. What fool would pass up a chance with a beautiful and intelligent woman like Sarah? Only one fool – ME!' he thought cursing under his breath. He decided that at least he needs to go in and apologize for the way he acted and hopefully she will find room in her heart to forgive him. He got out of the car and headed for the house.

Sarah was not her usual self when she got in the house and her mother could tell something was very wrong:

"Sarah, what is the matter? You look as if you saw a ghost – haah!"

"Yes Mum, I saw a ghost – Shungu" she said pacing up and down.

"But I thought that is what you wanted so that you could confront him and finally find closure and move on. Didn't you say that until you spoke to him face to face you were not going to get married? So did you talk to him?" She asked expressionlessly.

"No Mum, when I saw him I was so angry I could not talk to him but I have a feeling I am going to see him again" she said and went on to explain about Kuda being in hospital and her being one of the nurses attending to him.

"Life is full of twists and turns, who could have thought a man that hated you so much is now depending on your care" her mother said with a chuckle. She went on:

"Some of these things happen for a reason, God knew you needed to see Shungu and so he brought him to you through his brother – don't you see?" she concluded.

"Mum, how can you say that, this hurts more that when he rejected me because now I will get to see his family when they come to visit Kuda and that will hurt even more – don't you see. As for my children what do I tell them if he decides he does not want to have anything to do with them? She said choking.

"Well, it's time you told him and get his reaction once and for all, hopefully you will get another chance to see him at the hos . . ." she was interrupted by a knock on the door. Sarah went to the bathroom because she thought it was a neighbor and she didn't want them to see her crying. Her mother got up and opened the door. She recognized Shungu immediately and he recognized her too. Shungu did not need to utter any words, the pain in his eyes was enough for her to just invite him in:

"Sarah! Sarah, Shungu is here to see you" She called out announcing the visitor so as to prepare herself before she walked in. Sarah thought 'this is it, it's now or never' She went to her children's room and told them to come and meet their father. Benjamin nearly ran past her to the living room but she grabbed hold of him and held one in each hand then walked in trying so hard not to break down. Shungu stood up and their eyes met, it felt like the first time they first looked in each other's eyes. The lock was broken by Benjamin who asked:

"So Mum is this our father?" Still looking at Shungu she nodded.

<hr />

So many things happen for a reason in life and what is meant to be will surely come to pass. My parents were meant to be together no matter what – the flame of their love was still burning inside and did not need much kindling. This enduring love was unique - who could have thought such love would exist between Spinach and Nhamo's children? It is true that God works in mysterious ways.

My father felt that God gave him a second chance with a woman who not only brings him joy but has given him the most important gifts of all – the five children, namely, Gladys, Emmanuel (Benjamin), Dorothy (that's me), Andrew and Jane. Benjamin and Gladys were so spoiled because I think my father was still trying to make up for the eight years lost. As for my mother (Sarah) she was and is still treated like a Queen she is.

Uncle Kuda (Garikayi) succumbed to HIV/AIDS and unfortunately did not have any children of his own. My father is the sole survivor in the Nhamo clan and hopefully Benjamin and Andrew will carry the flag forward.

CHECK OUT THE NEW BOOK OF MY LIFE – YOU DON'T WANNAH MISS IT, YOU THINK THIS STORY WAS TWISTED? WAIT UNTIL YOU READ MY STORY...

www.ingramcontent.com/pod-product-compliance
Lightning Source LLC
Chambersburg PA
CBHW021231280526
45784CB00005B/2059